How to Do a Company Plan
and Put it into Action

a step-by-step guide for managers

By the same author (in conjunction with G. J. Day)

The Businessman's Complete Checklist

How to Do a Company Plan and Put it into Action

a step-by-step guide for managers

W. C. Shaw

BUSINESS BOOKS

London Melbourne Sydney Auckland Johannesburg

Business Books Ltd
An imprint of the Hutchinson Publishing Group
17–21 Conway Street, London W1P 6JD

Hutchinson Group (Australia) Pty Ltd
30–32 Cremorne Street, Richmond South, Victoria 3121
PO Box 151, Broadway, New South Wales 2007

Hutchinson Group (NZ) Ltd
32–34 View Road, PO Box 40–086, Glenfield, Auckland 10

Hutchinson Group (SA) (Pty) Ltd
PO Box 337, Bergvlei 2012, South Africa

First published 1981
Reprinted 1982, 1983

© W. C. Shaw 1981

Set in Univers

Printed in Great Britain by The Anchor Press Ltd
and bound by Wm Brendon & Son Ltd
both of Tiptree, Essex

British Library Cataloguing in Publication Data
Shaw, W.C.
How to do a company plan and put it into action
1. Management
2. Planning
I. Title
658.4′01   HD38
ISBN 0 09 145980 X

Contents

(A full contents list for each Unit is given immediately after the Introduction to the Unit.)

Introduction

Effective management necessitates the search for answers to questions and the solution to problems. The fact that problems exist is often obscure but until problems are identified the opportunities to apply remedial action are limited.

The Businessman's Complete Checklist, the companion work, is designed to help management ask questions – it is a management primer; *a catalyst for action*. So often the obvious is missed in the pressure of modern business. With *The Businessman's Complete Checklist* the owner, manager, consultant and student has access to a book with a logical approach to the structure of the majority of businesses, large or small – the fundamental principles being the same.

Problem-solving necessitates a level of competence in the field of business – whether manufacturing, marketing, understanding and using financial information or motivating people – competence that is difficult to acquire evenly across the many disciplines affecting business.

Time and money are valuable resources to dissipate, hence a condensed everyday approach to the solution of problems is required – a practical approach in layman's language. *How to Do a Company Plan and Put it into Action* is just that, providing step-by-step practical action points, prompted by soundly based principles. The Units are arranged in logical sequence:

UNIT 1 *How to do a company plan* The formation of a company plan, the identification of product and company strengths and weaknesses and the translation of the plan into action.

UNIT 2 *How to plan and control business* A structured approach to business profitability and efficiency and the introduction and practice of business disciplines in a manufacturing and assembly environment.

UNIT 3 *How to present management information efficiently as an input to Units 1 and 2* Building an effective corporate plan depends on an efficient management information system. This unit provides ideas on the varying use of management information layouts and effective aids to business control.

The questions posed in the text are answered in a positive and straightforward manner to be used by management at all levels. Because of the simplicity of the solutions suggested, little additional experience is required other than a sound commonsense approach.

How to Do a Company Plan and Put it into Action is a complete work and its cost should be recovered quickly by anyone who uses its practical and proven approach.

For the consultant and business student the book provides a degree of practice not usually found in management books – the case studies are set against the pressures of modern business where the planning horizon is in reality not more than 18 months to 2 years.

Throughout the book is the acceptance of 'people' problems and solutions, taking account of accepted principles of management.

1

Caveat

The business scene is ever-changing and one of management's primary responsibilities is to anticipate and respond to changes in the economy and the external pressures upon the enterprise.

Because of these changing conditions, it is difficult in a planning and action textbook of this kind to take account of possible future changes and still retain the credibility of the models. The assumptions in the case studies are based on a general set of assumptions with a fit nearest to current economic conditions. You must ensure that authentic plans take account of the conditions ruling at the time of preparation.

In order to maintain this credibility further, it was decided to use calendar years in the models in place of a form of alphanumeric numbering. It is intended that this will retain the feeling of reality.

How to use and get maximum benefit from 'How to Do a Company Plan and Put it into Action'

The practical examples are designed to assist readers to obtain the maximum benefit quickly. No two readers will have the same approach nor the same level of expertise. The following will, however, be helpful as introductory background.

UNIT 1: Corporate planning

Sound and practical planning is the essence of business and means asking questions such as:
  Are we satisfying or creating a market?
  Where is the market for the products we sell? Is this market expanding or shrinking? If the latter –
  What new products or ventures can be established to ensure that efficiency and profitability are maintained or increased?
  Will the company be over-resourced with resultant costs affecting its financial stability and its future? Are projected finances sufficient for the company's plans?

Judgement plays an important part in the daily management decision-taking process but there are many occasions where these judgements must be supported by a logical analysis of the problem and a quantification of the assembled facts and assumptions. This quantification validates management hunch.

Every business requires a plan against which its management can focus action and measure achievements. That plan is the scenario against which the day-to-day operations will perform. The more complex or diverse the company is, the greater is the requirement for a plan to highlight and take account of the many interactions within the total operation. Unit 1 shows how a corporate plan is built up, taking you step by step through the planning process in a company – the Functional Chair Manufacturing Company.

What would have been the outcome of the company had the planning process of *Functional Chair Manufacturing* not identified in advance that:

1 The sales force required reorganisation to meet the challenge of more demanding targets (Section 3.1)
2 Cost and scarcity of hardwood in the next two years will cause increased use of veneer and synthetic laminates (Section 4.3).
3 A major breakthrough is expected in the next two years; moulded plastic will have a texture similar to wood (Section 4.3).
4 The sales value and volume of wooden chairs, one of the company's major lines, was projected to fall substantially over a period of five years (Section 5.2).
5 An employee motivation programme was urgently required (Section 7.1).
6 The investment in fixed assets (factory space and plant and other equipment) would increase from £470,000 at the end of the planned first year to a level of £1,820,000 by the end of the plan's fifth year (Section 5.4).
7 To support projected growth, bank borrowings would have to rise from the present

2

level of £400,000 to £820,000 over a period of five years (Section 5.4).

Every business has its own key facts which it must identify. A quantified plan translates management's objectives into manageable areas of action whereby tasks can be assigned to individuals.

Corporate planning simply means asking the questions. Where is the organisation going? How is it going to get there? How long will the journey take? These identify the specific areas which require management action to strengthen the existing strong points and eliminate the weak ones. This remedial action, coupled with a balancing of total resources, leads to good management practice and a soundly based, professionally motivated business.

The example plan identifies, by a process of expertise and challenge, those areas which, when remedied or improved, could affect the overall performance and return on capital within an acceptable planning horizon (which can be shorter or longer as required) and the company's projected financial base. What is important is the structured and disciplined review of the total organisation. Corporate plans, such as the example in Unit 1, are constructed from the lowest decision-taking level in the organisation and moved upwards through the structure to reflect the accountability of management. Top-down planning is invariably over-optimistic and increases the possibility of dangerous gaps in the total plan.

The majority of 'first-time round' plans require reshaping and pruning to fit the available or projected resources. For example, there is little point in planning to sell articles which cannot be manufactured or bought-in and require working capital support beyond the amount that is likely to be available to the company.

A plan that emerges without doubts or guesstimates first-time round should be viewed with suspicion.

The corporate plan of *Functional Chair Manufacturing* is an example of the requirement within a company which is already geared to operate using an effective management information system related to well developed and tested management attitudes. Not all corporate plans require to be so complex but each must be tailored to the needs of management so that the probability of achieving the agreed objectives can be assessed against the effects of both internal and external constraints. What is happening to the national economy within a country of operation must, ultimately, affect its business community. Assimilating the trends within a plan and the recognition of the possible effect during the span of the planning process is essential for meaningful, realistic and flexible planning.

The guidelines to follow in order to achieve a meaningful plan are as follows:

- Review or lay down the company's objectives – probably the most important step in the planning exercise.
- Assess past or present performance against these objectives.
- Lay down clear instructions for the preparation of the plan to ensure that a consistent approach will be maintained at all levels.
- Consolidate the plan and examine the short-term requirements in relation to the longer term.
- Test the plan for errors or omissions and against existing or projected resources.
- Refine the plan by a recycling process through the same management track from which it originated.
- Agree and adopt the plan and assign accountable action tasks to individuals.
- Incorporate the plan into management information routines and ensure that progress can be monitored.
- Set reporting and action monitoring timetables to review progress and to revise the plan where necessary.

A step-by-step guide to the process of corporate planning is set out in Unit 1 and to enable the reader to acquire an overview of the total process the diagram overleaf will be helpful.

CORPORATE PLANNING CYCLE

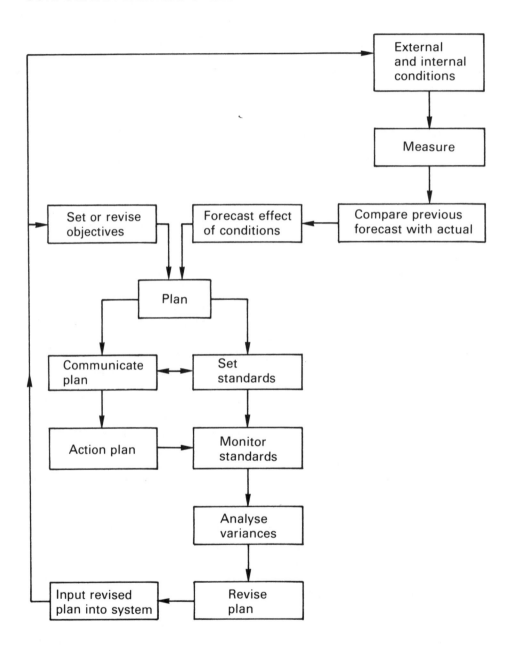

UNIT 2: Company overhaul

What of the company which has not developed, no matter the reason, the level of its management disciplines, its management information systems and the effectiveness of its financial controls. There are many such companies which operate profitably apparently on a day-to-day decision-taking basis, but how can maximum potential be measured, not only in terms of profitability, but in human terms of task achievement if yardsticks are not established to stretch both the organisation and its workforce.

It is in times of company stress in a confused trading environment that the company with the more disciplined approach may be better able to weather these difficulties.

Leisure Sound Limited, the company example in Unit 2, found itself in a situation of thwarted expectation. The non-realisation of management hopes provided the motivation for a change in style and the desire to introduce a sense of professionalism; to achieve aspirations; turning hopes into reality. First it was necessary to introduce a measure of direction and control.

Overhaul of any organisation in circumstances of this kind is not difficult but it requires the obvious to be stated – the overhaul must start at the beginning. A company, like an engine, must be tuned to ensure that there is no dissipation of resources with the component parts working in unison. Some companies have a yearly overhaul; some manage to see the exercise as a continuous process.

The basic questions are: How is the company doing now? Is there room for improvement? How can a company plan for and monitor this process? These questions, in turn, must lead the company to ask the fundamental questions: What can we expect at the end of the day? Why are we in business? What are our company objectives? The answers are the essence of the overhaul process.

The key steps in this process – valid for every company – are traced in Unit 2 through the example of *Leisure Sound*.

Where is the company going, and why? is asked by *Leisure Sound's* management. Profits are short of expectation and the prospect of refusal by the company's bankers to support increased borrowing requirements had to be faced (Section 1.5).

The lack of objectives or management guidelines had to be remedied first. The main objectives are set out in Section 4.2.

The elements of the overhaul have been agreed previously by function (areas of responsibility) namely, Management, Marketing, Production and Accounting, the questions basic to the business being set down for answer in Section 3. These questions will prompt others from which an overall analysis of the company and its strengths and weaknesses will emerge. The next stage is the preparation of a plan, the simple guidelines for which are listed in Section 4.

Each functional area of the business is examined after assigning job responsibility to individuals. A redesigned factory layout forms the basis of a revised costing and control system and enables decisions on product volume and flow to be fed into the plan, which, when finally prepared, will cover similar ground to that in Unit 1 but more immediate and less complicated.

The procedure from there on is the same as that for the acceptance and introduction of the corporate plan for *Functional Chair Manufacturing* shown in detail in Unit 1.

The process of company overhaul must not stop when the plan is complete. The process should be continuous, it is only the formal review which takes place at pre-determined intervals of time. Unit 2 shows you how.

UNIT 3

As management style is personal to each individual so is the manner in which information is presented. Unit 3 consists of different forms of data presentation covering graphs and the more traditional standard columnar method. Invariably, information requirements grow and forms get larger to accommodate the greater volume of data. Existing information is seldom scrutinised to determine what is superfluous. The hidden cost of producing volumes of unnecessary data is considerable and must be reviewed periodically.

Management at all levels must have the necessary information to manage and discharge their accountability. The form of presentation of this information is a matter of personal choice; it is the content which matters and it is up to the manager to state what information he needs and in what form.

The examples show varying ways in which data may be presented so as to give only essential management information which the manager needs to function effectively. Superfluous information needs to be cut out as it is a waste of time and resources – both for the person preparing it and the manager who has to use it.

Unit 3 shows you how information can be presented effectively.

The author and publishers would like to thank Harry Jones and Gower Publishing Company Limited for permission to reproduce material as follows from Mr Jones's book *Preparing Company Plans*, published in 1974 by Gower:

Data Sheet 8   Consolidated Control Sheet
Data Sheet 13   Sales Planning: Annual Totals
Data Sheet 14   Summary of Capital Employed
Data Sheet 15   Fixed Assets Budget
Data Sheet 16   Projected Capital Expenditure
Data Sheet 17   Capital Projects: Planning Production Capacity
Date Sheet 18   Current Assets Budget
Data Sheet 23   Information Base for Financial Resources
Data Sheet 24   Summary of Sources and Use of Funds
Data Sheet 38   Summary of Salient Management Information

How to do a company plan

The pace of economic change today is such that to operate a business enterprise, large or small, without a forward plan is imprudent. Change is forced on a business by measures often completely outside the control of its executives, who have, nevertheless, the responsibility to anticipate change in the first place – an almost 'heads you win, tails I lose' situation.

The enterprise run on *ad hoc* expedient or opportunist decision-taking lines has a difficult task to remain a long-term viable entity. Problems of solvency escalate when trading conditions arise such as those experienced recently in the United Kingdom and elsewhere.

'Disasters strike other people' is a popular belief but with little logical basis. If this was true there would be little necessity for the purchase of insurance cover.

Planning is a form of insurance, on the one hand against failure or collapse of the enterprise, on the other to ensure that opportunities are identified and the benefits arising from these are maximised through the evaluation today of the probable conditions in which the enterprise will trade tomorrow.

Planning ahead is concerned with the answers to four questions:

Where does the enterprise stand now?
What are the objectives for the future?
How are these objectives to be achieved?
What decisions must be taken now?

The identification of the present position of the enterprise in terms of its strengths and weaknesses, its products and its resources, is fundamental to the evaluation of any forward planning. It is the base line of the plan without which any plan is valueless. By stating the present at the commencement of the planning exercise, close scrutiny of the obvious is possible.

The development of the corporate plan for *Functional Chair Manufacturing* starts with the present and takes the reader through a logical process, searching for answers to the four questions above to a degree dependent on the information available from the company's management information system.

As the success of the enterprise depends on the interrelationship of its various functions, so does the future plan. The simulated plan that follows covers marketing, new product development, property availability, personnel, finance and management generally. In other words, effective planning stems from:

A knowledge of the enterprise and its markets.
Use of the information and planning system.
Co-ordination.
Creative thinking.
Choice of different options.

The route along which the enterprise will

proceed depends on the objectives set by its proprietors or management. The attainment of these objectives will depend upon the attitude to customers and employees; change inside or outside the enterprise and the degree of risk-taking, the financial consequences stemming from the plan and the effectiveness of converting short- and long-term plans into a course of action. A planning system that has no built-in mechanism to ensure that conversion will not succeed.

The example plan deals with the manufacture of chairs; small, large, wooden, metal, inexpensive and expensive. The systematic approach can be used for any enterprise, large or small, and any form of product. The principles are valid.

The Functional Chair
Manufacturing Company Limited

Development of a Corporate Plan
Five-year Sales, Profit and Facilities
Plan Commencing 1982

Contents of Unit 1

4 The plan's assumptions

5 Objectives

6-10 Final details

Summary of contents

The following profit plan represents a step-by-step approach to the planning process. Where are you. Where you want to go. How you want to travel. When do you want to arrive. Who is going to drive. How much you want to pay for the trip. In using this step-by-step approach to plan for areas of responsibility, a series of statements relating to each question will be made. BE simple. State and use the information required to make decisions.

EXECUTIVE SUMMARY

Starting point:
1 *Business function* What are you here for? Your purpose or mission.
2 *Environment/competition* What are the factors affecting your ability to do the job?
3 *Capabilities/opportunities* Your strengths and weaknesses plus your course of action.

Where you want to get:
4 *Assumptions/potentials* What you should anticipate about the future.
5 *Objectives/goals* Selecting a target.

Travel method:
6 *Policies/procedures* The way in which you do things.
7 *Programmes/projects* The heart of operational planning – what has to be done.

Time of arrival:
8 *Priorities/schedules* Timetable on projects.

Leader:
9 *Organisation/delegation* People planning.

Costs involved:
10 *Budgets/resources* Costing out the course of action.

PLANNING — THE CORPORATE ENTITY

STRATEGIC

INTERNAL

Review company objectives
Assess achievements & strengths & weaknesses

EXTERNAL

Assess political economic legislative competitive environment

Revise objectives: profitability market share return on capital personnel social

Evaluate action options

Define strategic plan

TACTICAL

SHORT TERM

LONG TERM

Company Structure

Style of management
Business sector
Location
Diversification

Resources

Human
Finance
Facilities
Divestment

Products

Materials
Marketing
Research
Development

1 Nature of business

1.1 GENERAL

The Functional Chair Manufacturing Company (FCM) is engaged in the business of manufacturing and marketing at a profit speciality furniture for use in conference rooms and small halls.

The aim is to provide
- A moderate range of exclusive designs and services
- through a direct sales force
- selling to both commercial and private customers.

The company was incorporated in 1968 and has had promising growth each year.

In 1976, agreements were reached between FCM and a Swedish firm to manufacture and sell a line of stainless steel and wooden furniture.

A separate direct sales division was formed in 1975, Scandia Products, operating in competition with National Direct Sales. The majority of the metalwork in chair and table frames is sub-contracted.

1.2 OPERATING PHILOSOPHY

FCM adheres to the following beliefs:

Equality of opportunity for all men and women regardless of race, colour, or creed.

The right of each individual to political and religious freedom, exercised with responsibility.

The principle that all types of business can operate more successfully under the free enterprise system with private management and competition.

The role of democratic government to preserve the rights of the individual citizen with a minimum of restriction and interference.

Each individual's responsibility to develop and utilise his capacity for maximum achievement.

The company's responsibility to so conduct its affairs that it is held in high esteem in each community in which it is located.

1.3 BASIC MANAGERIAL BELIEFS

1.4 MARKETS/CUSTOMERS

The following basic managerial beliefs guide the management and employees of FCM in their functions:

To create, stimulate and satisfy customers.

To maintain and develop the best possible morale among its employees.

To provide the opportunity for advancement for all who earn it by superior performance.

To maintain the facilities so that they contribute to the attractiveness of the neighbourhood.

To conduct the business so as to promote and protect the free enterprise system.

To engage in social and charitable work in the community.

	Sales volume 1981, %
Corporate customers	29
Local and national government	18
Private clubs and associations	17
Hotels	12
Other	11
Business schools	8
Private individuals	3
Universities	2
	100

FCM customers require furniture with the following features:

1 Comfort; so as to avoid fatigue.
2 Appealing design, often exclusive or custom.
3 Above average durability.
4 Minimum maintenance, consistent with materials used.

They also require, in many cases, advice on furnishing and environment.

Chairs:
  Wooden
  Wooden, upholstered
  Wooden, upholstered, posture
  Metal, upholstered
  Metal, upholstered, posture

Tables:
  Wooden
  Wooden, inlaid
  Wooden, scratch-resistant
  Wooden and metal

Buffet, occasional tables:
  Wooden
  Wooden, scratch-resistant

Services:
  Furnishing and decorating advice
  Supervision of installation
  Refinishing

Marketing and sales:
  Research
  Market
  Customer loyalty
  Competition activity
  Advertising

Products:
  Standards
  Design
  Customer requirements
  New products

Manufacturing:
  Production methods
  Workload planning
  New methods
  Materials control

Administrative:
  Accounting
  Activity control
  Cost control
  Personnel
  Legal: patents

General research:

How does marketing research expenditure compare with competitors?
What marketing research has been accomplished in home and export markets?
How effective was it?
Are efficient information services available?
What data is there available?
What methods of marketing research have been found to be effective?
What experimentation is taking place?
Are independent agencies preferred to inhouse researchers?
How can product intelligence be obtained?

Market research:

Total size of market
Rate of change of size
Factors affecting changes
Number of competitors
Competitors' market share
Competitors' change in market share
Competitors' sales organisation structure
Ruling current market prices
Forecasts of market conditions
Seasonal/cyclical market fluctuations
Market potential (new and existing)
User characteristics/attitudes/opinions
Potential customers – kind, number and location
Product uses
Customers' product selection criteria, e.g. performance, size, shape, service
Sources of customer dissatisfaction
Competitive position of company products
Distribution methods

1.7.2 Factors influencing market-share checklist

Customer loyalty:

How many suppliers to customer?
How long have they been?
Rate of change of suppliers?
Rate of change of business between suppliers?
How easy is it to change?

Suppliers' image:

Product attributes
  quality
  performance
  reliability
  appearance
  price
  ease of maintenance
  full range

Suppliers' attributes:
  reliable delivery
  quick delivery
  technical service and advice
  attention to complaints
  order handling
  credit terms and discounts
  commercial services

Competition activity:

Increasing/decreasing
Product comparison
Pricing
Availability

Market-share ratios:

Cost per £x sales
Cost per customer serviced
Cost per sales transaction
Cost per £x gross contribution
Average selling cost per unit
Selling prices
Discount structures
Relative sales mixes
Gross/net contribution per representative
Gross/net contribution per sales area
Gross/net contribution per distribution area
Gross/net contribution per order
Administration costs (sales)

1.7.3 Advertising checklist

Types of media:

Newspapers
Trade papers
Television
Radio
Cinema
Subscription journals
Business supplements
Posters
Placards
Direct mail
Exhibitions
Educational campaigns
Export journals
Institute publications
Other publications

Reason for use:

Changes opinions and attitudes – level of change depends on frequency and quality
Market share depends on opinions of product
Significantly improves level of sales closings (especially where no regular customer contact)
Reduced costs of selling – if adequate frequency
Advertising in well advertised markets increases cost of selling

Allocation of funds:

Existing production capacity
Saturation point where resources become limited or expensive
Rate of market response to extra sales and marketing effort
Future market growth potential
Use contribution figures after direct costs instead of sales figures
Use true gross profit to net profit monetary values instead of % figures (relieves the considerable confusion created thereby)

Cost product groups down to net profit contribution (show marketing support costs in each group)

Media strategy:

Is the market horizontal (everybody) or vertical (selective)?
Where the primary objective of a press campaign is to enhance the reputation of the advertiser, large spaces in horizontal media are most likely to succeed.
When the primary objective is enquiries, small spaces in vertical media are usually more appropriate, particularly where a reader reply service is operated by the publisher.
Where the application of the product has distinct operational benefits, case histories are often most effective.
Where advantages are in the price/delivery/quality areas, a generalised customer-benefit approach is appropriate.

Measuring effectiveness:

Aim:
  to make advertising work harder and more effectively
  to use professional and creative people
Do not:
  assume you know your present and potential customers
  use a publication or programme just because you like it
  approach advertising with preconceived ideas
  produce advertising that just pleases your boss
  forget it is the effects of advertising that are most important – these must be measured

1.7.4 New product planning requirements checklist

Business strategy is expressed in products.

Product programmes are the foundation of forward company planning.

The new product programme is a top management responsibility.

The new product function should be organised as a top executive staff function, headed by a person who can work effectively at top management level.

Organisation and control should be established in conformance with the stages of new product evolution:

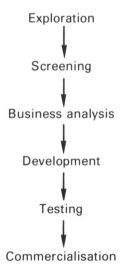

Exploration

↓

Screening

↓

Business analysis

↓

Development

↓

Testing

↓

Commercialisation

Co-ordinated new product effort is best achieved through interdepartmental product teams, representing all functional areas of the business, tailored to fit the characteristics of each product.

A definite programme, carefully planned and closely managed, significantly improves new product results.

New idea creation can be directed and controlled to achieve improved pertinence and quality of product ideas.

New product selection is accomplished by a continuing series of evaluations in all stages. No single screening is adequate.

Selection standards for products to be developed should be upgraded persistently to achieve an ever-increasing yield from available manpower and resources.

Product planning requires adequate specifications and a programme for each product prior to laboratory development.

Market requirements and opportunities are the primary consideration in product planning.

Company acquisition should be integrated with internal development to achieve a balanced new product programme.

1.7.5 New product acquisition checklist

How strong is the product range of company X?

Are competitors likely to become more effective in the near future?

Are the markets for the products of company X growing or declining? How and why?

Will company X still be successful for the foreseeable future?

Stages in product acquisition:

exploration
screening
investigation
proposition
negotiation
integration

Key pitfalls:

Not placing responsibility at a sufficiently high level
Failing to establish a real unanimity of opinion as to what the acquisition objectives should be
Setting unrealistic criteria for today's competitive sellers' market
Searching only among companies for sale
Failing to recognise the time required for a successful acquisition programme
Failing to focus the search correctly
Failing to investigate prior to actual negotiations
Failing to assess correctly a seller's motives
Overlooking opportunities by using mechanical screening procedures
Failure to obtain qualified outside assistance when needed
Too much analysis and too little action; or *vice versa*

Success criteria:

To establish clearly defined growth objectives
Sound internal organisation to establish acquisition criteria

1.7.6 General manufacturing checklist

Do adequate standards exist?

Are performance records adequate?

Are variances promptly reported and fully investigated?

If some employees perform both direct and indirect activities, is the system for distinguishing the time spent on each adequate?

Are all processing operations necessary?

Could alternative processes be used to advantage?

Could existing processes be simplified?

Is the sequence of operations the best possible?

Is idle time between operations at a minimum?

Can operations be performed in different departments to avoid handling delays?

Do any operations result in excessive rejects?

Are required completion dates shown on production orders?

In scheduling production is sufficient lead time allowed to enable the accumulation of small orders?

Are set-up costs minimised by allowing sufficient lead time?

Can labour be scheduled more efficiently with long production lead times?

Can special processing requirements be fitted in, with a sufficiently small lead time?

Are alternative processing methods developed and used for scheduling standard operations in bottleneck areas?

Are cost differences between alternate processing methods known?

Are machine loadings used for production scheduling?

Are workloads planned sufficiently far in advance to permit workforce and machines to be balanced?

How much idle time and overtime occurred in the previous period/year?

How much was anticipated?

How much subcontracting was done last year?

Why was this required?

Is scrap/spoilage a significant element of production cost?

Is there a sound procedure for disposing of scrap?

Is scrap sold on the basis of bids?

Are records of spoilage maintained for control purposes?

Are all categories of cost in the manufacturing sphere planned in advance?

Are these the specified responsibility of named individuals?

Does the company employ a flexible budgeting procedure?

Is the inventory of maintenance spares adequate?

Are shortages excessive in the light of the total investment?

Are supply costs of consumable production materials properly isolated from general maintenance costs?

Are supplies purchased in economic quantities?

Are there safeguards against overstocking?

Do excessive material shortages arise?

Are obsolete supplies disposed of?

Is there adequate protection against pilferage and wastage?

Are containers compatible with storage, and materials handling?

Is the most suitable materials handling equipment used?

Can materials be moved best by gravity or on rollers?

Is a conveyor justified?

Are fork-lift trucks and pallets used to advantage?

Are the materials handling and manufacturing functions effectively co-ordinated?

Where should incoming and outgoing materials be located with respect to work stations?

Can operations be combined at one work station to reduce materials handling?

Are containers uniform to permit stacking?

Can palletised loads be used?

Could lighter or low-cost packaging be used?

Is shrink wrapping possible with current advance in technology?

Is packaging design co-ordinated with materials handling?

Do all items really need packages?

Are scrap and waste materials dealt with effectively?

Are containers marked/coloured for easier segregation/identification?

Could materials be purchased in sizes or quantities that would make for easier materials handling?

How much capital is tied up in obsolete materials/components?

Could excess stocks be sold in bulk with special discounts, or is it cheaper to allow high stocks to run down through normal usage?

How much of inventory investment is in work-in-progress?

What are the costs of carrying each type of inventory?

What are the costs of reordering items for inventory?

Are order points developed for each item on the basis of lead times, rates of usage, and safety stocks?

If of value, are returnable containers properly accounted for and controlled?

Could a deposit system be used for returnable containers/pallets?

Are incoming goods examined for quantity, quality and conformance to order?

Has an analysis been carried out to verify lead times used in reordering?

Where sales are seasonal is it more advisable to produce in accordance with demand, or to produce at an even rate, and use stocks as a buffer?

What is management accounting?

It is the interpretation of financial data for the purposes of day-to-day management control and decision-taking

It uses the same data base as for financial accounting
It relates the present to previous plans
It is unaffected by statutory requirements relating to presentation of accounting information
It takes account of the management structure in terms of individual accountability and responsibility
It is the data recording process within the management information system

How does it operate?

Budgets form a part of the management information system
Actual results are compared with budgets
Budgets are updated when necessary in the form of forecasts

What does a management accounting system include?

Routine accounting statements to show budget compared with actual profit
Balance sheet
Cash flow
Capital expenditure
Volumes manufactured and sold
Performance ratios
Variance statement

Can it be eliminated without much harm to the results?

Does it cost more than it is worth?

Can it be reduced in scope and cost?

Does it do more than is required?

Can it be done more cheaply another way?

Can it be done more cheaply by someone else?

Is there an alternative service from outside which is adequate but cheaper?

Can the service or expenses supporting the operation be reduced?

On a management judgement basis, can the operation be sensibly considered to provide its full share of overhead and net profit contribution?

How does it affect other costs in the business?

If you were to start the business again would you include it?

1.7.10 Cost control checklist

Does the cost control system have the active backing of top management?

Do controls conform to the organisation structures?

Is the system seen as being an essential part of the company's management process?

Are responsible individuals aware of the need to plan their activities?

Do those individuals charged with various costs really have control over these costs?

Are cost controls established according to the nature of the tasks?

Do all who require it receive cost information?

Do responsible individuals who are held accountable play a full role in setting cost levels?

Is cost control information geared to the requirements of responsible individuals?

Is the costing system adequate in general terms?

Do control reports cover both financial and related causal factors?

Are cost control requirements and reports discussed with recipients?

Does the basis of measuring desired performance reflect those aspects of output and input that are important?

Is the principle of management by exception followed?

Are results measured in accordance with the same units of measure in which the standards are set?

Do recipients of control information know how to extract the most essential facts?

Are controls flexible and economical in operation?

Are deviations reported rapidly?

Do controls help to explain variances and to indicate the corrective action that is required?

Are control reports brief, simple to read, and relevant?

Are actions taken on the basis of these reports?

Are control reports used to indicate relative efficiencies?

Do all employees understand the cost implications of their work?

Do all employees have cost targets?

Do the benefits of the cost control system outweigh its costs?

Are unnecessary reports eliminated, and are new ones introduced only when clearly needed?

Is the control system revised each time an organisational change takes place?

Do good relations exist between the accounting staff and line management?

Offices and manufacturing facilities in Yorkshire, England

	Area, ft^2	Total area, ft^2
Manufacturing plant:		
Machine shop	8,500	
Glue shop	7,000	
Finishing and upholstery shop	12,000	27,500
Storage:		
Covered	5,000	
Yard	3,500	8,500
Warehouse	3,000	3,000
Offices	2,000	2,000
		_____
Total space available		41,000
		_____

2 Economic background

2.1 ENVIRONMENT — GENERAL

2.1.1 Environment checklist

The general business environment is cautious.

High inflationary spiral of previous years is seen as stabilising and at the end of two years containable in single figures.

A shortage of materials coupled with a high demand for machine tools.

Shortage of skilled labour, technical, managerial and clerical staff.

General labour unrest; industrial disputes and strikes increasing.

Many companies lacking liquidity through the erosion of the capital base during inflationary period.

Deferred and essential capital expenditure projects analysed critically.

Indication of new project starts.

Easing of demands on taxation system and control of inflation leaving higher spendable income in individual hands.

Increasing investment in leisure, both outside and inside the home.

Are all resources effectively utilised?

Attitude of individuals to health and safety.

Effects of pollution on health.

The effects of world recession on company's products and raw materials.

Buying pattern for home.

Standard of living.

Technological and design innovations.

Volume of products completing their profit cycle.

How critical is senior management about the adequacy of the company's operation?

Is information on external conditions (as they might affect the company) reported in the management information?

Know where facts stop and assumptions begin.

2.2 GROWTH OF INDUSTRY — GENERAL

2.2.1 Growth of industry checklist

The domestic and commercial furniture market has grown most rapidly between 1971 and 1974, due to record levels of personal income and industrial production. This has been reflected in the construction and modernisation of offices, private clubs and civic centres.

Declining profits in 1978 and 1979 have caused cost-reduction programmes in industry and the cutback in capital spending generally will seriously affect the commercial furniture market throughout 1980 and 1981 into 1982.

Similar trends are expected in the domestic market.

The rising costs and shortage of hardwood has been a major problem, but has stimulated developments in synthetics and furniture manufacturing techniques.

Does senior management possess a sound knowledge of the company and its markets?

How successful has the company been in creating demand as opposed to satisfying demand?

Is the search for new business opportunities structural or by chance?

Is the company's management creative?

Does the company manufacture to someone else's specification and design?

Has a substantial market ever arisen from one-off 'specials'?

Capability of the sales organisation.

Unrecognisable patterns.

Cycles: economic, seasonal.

FCM is in an extremely competitive field. The competition can be classified into three main groups:

1 The large furniture companies such as
    Sitrite
    Quality Veneer
    Exquisite Wood
  who have excellent facilities and production potential but can compete with FCM only in cost. They do not provide the attention and quality of product and service that FCM offer. They share equally a major part of the hotel business.

2 The small companies that are similar in operation to FCM are the greatest threat. There are many such companies, with the same potential, and it is by offering superior service that FCM aim to keep ahead of this group.

3 The small carpenter, who competes strongly on a local basis but who does not have the facility to sell or supply to chain-operated or High Street groups.

Is slow response to competitors' activity a managable problem?

What is the effect and trend in competition from overseas?

Competitors' strengths and weaknesses in pricing policies.

Promotional activity.

Patent restrictions.

Sophistication of service levels.

Today's and tomorrow's winners.

Problem exploitation.

Is the new product programme a top management responsibility?

Market requirements and opportunities are the primary considerations in product planning.

Do competitors control or influence the supply of raw materials?

The Woodworkers and Crafts Union won the right to represent the bargaining unit in May 1979, and an agreement covering a period of two years was negotiated in October 1979, expiring October 1981.

There have been no work stoppages.

There have been no 'closed shop' demands.

Can the parameters of worker participation be defined?

Should participation be encouraged?

Are employees motivated?

Are employees' rewards directly related to performance?

How much involvement should employees have?

How is the social value of the individual measured?

What are 'reasonable working conditions'?

What adjustments are required to change industry on to a democratic basis?

Are the problems associated with union sensitivity sufficient to pioneer and anticipate?

Effect of increasing demand against pressure for shorter hours and less work.

Personal responsibility for community leadership.

3 Company analysis

Strengths	Weaknesses/problems	Action checklist

Market: chairs, wooden*

Customer satisfaction:

Strengths	Weaknesses/problems	Action checklist
Product quality	Sales coverage	Reorganise sales force
Service	Limited product line	Increase advertising budget
Reputation	Backlog of orders	Emphasise strengths
Experienced sales force	Price (needs intensive selling in some markets)	Continue customer orientation throughout the company

Productivity:

Strengths	Weaknesses/problems	Action checklist
Some good productive workers	High shipping costs	Investigate possibility of separate assembly shops
Uncomplicated product	Limited output	Plan expansion programme
	High manufacturing cost of quality product	Cost reduction programme
	New employees of low calibre	Reorganise materials handling and storage
	Limited storage space	
	Limited work space	

Innovation:

Strengths	Weaknesses/problems	Action checklist
Marketing ideas	Customers are generally opposed to new ideas in design	Arrange training programme to keep abreast of technological development
Original furniture designs		
Some new chemical finishing techniques	Also employees	Better contact with the Wood Research Council

*Repeat this analysis for each product (where applicable) and service listed in Section 1.6

Strengths	Weaknesses/problems	Action checklist
Resources:		
People	Lack of permanent capital	Facilities improvement
Factory	Old machinery	Investigate new material
Finance	Lack of expansion space	sources
	Shortage of materials	
Management development and performance:		
Hard-working team	Lack organisation of their work-load	Profit planning programme
Well respected by their subordinates	Sales force spread too thinly	Management by objectives
Experienced team	Inadequate supervisory performance	Training programme
Employee attitude and performance:		
Good working climate and conditions	Inadequate fringe benefits	Induction programme needed
Above average pay rates	New employee attitude (do not identify themselves with the company)	Increase communications
Good union representation	Employees not aware of top management beliefs due to poor supervisory performance	Training programme in motivation for supervisor grade
Public responsibility:		
Above average facility surroundings	Financial contributions to charity limited	Encourage plant tours – contact schools and colleges
Many disabled workers	Limited product line	Sub-contract work to hospitals and larger institutions
Several employees engaged in civic duties		
No racial discrimination		

Continued

Strengths	Weaknesses/problems	Action checklist
Profitability:		
Low overheads	Limited facility	Analyse capital employed by product
Hard-working management and sales force	High labour content in product	
	Shortage of skilled labour	Set acceptable targets
Local employees	Reliance on intuitive management	Hold management seminars to explain financial policies
Debt/equity ratio acceptable		
Stock turnover average	Wide geographic market	Review management information systems
	Low return on capital employed	
	High investment in own stock in customers' departments	
	Low support from creditor finance	
Potential and profit:		
Large potential market	Customers in period of falling liquidity	Maintain activity in this market at about 20% of sales volume
	Most customers have cost-conscious buyers not impressed by quality	
	Moderate profit margin	
	Spending over next 18 months will be increased	
Advertising and selling:		
Executives are easy to reach	Difficult and costly to reach buyers through magazine media	Contact buyers personally and influence their future needs
Customers new building programme well publicised		Consider contacts with architects and design centres
	Customers want one service for all furniture needs	

Strengths	Weaknesses/problems	Action checklist

Competition:

| | Cannot compare cost-wise with large furniture manufacturing companies | Sell our products to large competitors – convince them of the advantages of a wider product range |
| | They have big accounts and can get repeat orders as they satisfy all the customer needs | |

Market: services

Quality/design:

Comfortable	Fabric not stain resistant	Test synthetic fabrics for comfort, etc.
	Complex design, too many parts	Redesign for cost reduction
	Customer complaints on loose leg rails	Review quality control

Production cost/price:

| | Excessive labour content in shaping and carving | Investigate three-axis machine tools. Justify capital expenditure |
| | Back requires excessive hand fitting on assembly | Review quality control and replace worn out tooling |

Marketing, effectiveness:

| Popular product | Old design | |
| Competitive price | | |

Action implementation is achieved by allotting the tasks to named individuals and setting personal standards as a tool for ensuring that action plans are converted into tasks which people can do – and are expected to do.

4 The plan's assumptions

4.1 GENERAL ASSUMPTIONS — SOCIO/POLITICAL

(1982 and five-year trend)

An 'assumption' is a temporary hypothesis regarding a very important future development which cannot be predicted with accuracy and over which there is no significant control.

International

Demand for goods and services in foreign markets will level off in 1982 but will increase substantially in next five years as result of economic growth, higher incomes in developing countries and increased international co-operation and the benefits arising from membership of the European Economic Community. Plans to enter this market must be formulated by mid-1982.

Domestic

Single *most important domestic political assumption* for five-year period is the *government's commitment* to revitalise the economy with continuing reduction in the unemployment level. This will have broad social, political and economic impact and will mean increased government planning and cash investment to combat recessions and promote stable, balanced economic growth with an acceptable level of employment.

Unemployment rate in 1982 will be less than 7% of the labour force and most types of labour (especially skilled labour) will be in short supply; unemployment rate in next five years will fluctuate between 7% and 5% of the labour force.

Income taxes (corporate and personal) *will be increased in 1981* as a 'temporary' anti-inflation move; after 1981 tax rates will possibly be reduced to current levels or lower.

Increased *pressure in labour relations field* during next five years (with general governmental support) *for increased worker security participation*, more job retaining by business and unions, and elimination of 'discriminatory' labour practices.

Population trend will have significant *impact on business* during next five years. Markets, especially, will reflect the increase (both in numbers and as percentage of population) of young people (more household formulations) and of elderly people (with more spendable income as result of Social Security increases).

(1982 – and five-year trend)

GNP* for 1981 is estimated to rise about 1% in current pounds or about 2% after adjustment for inflation; general economy will continue to grow (in real terms) at 1.5% p.a. in next five years.

Government spending will continue to increase each year during five-year period, particularly at local level for broad social welfare programme.

Business spending for plant and equipment over year will rise by up to 15% or more over 1981 and will decline to more sustainable levels in next five years.

Interest rates will be high but marginally below the record levels in 1979, reflecting exceptionally strong demand for funds and tight money-credit conditions; trend in rates will be moderately downward in next two years and stable thereafter.

During next five years, consumer demand will grow steadily more sophisticated, reflecting major economic and social changes taking place, e.g. larger disposable incomes, more leisure, better education, etc.

Cost and scarcity of hardwood will cause increased use of veneer and synthetic laminates.

By 1982 wooden furniture will drop to approximately 18% of the commercial market (currently 32%).

There will be techniques for applying veneer-type finishes to round and irregular surfaces within the next three years.

Synthetic fibres will be used increasingly in upholstery fabrics and be used in 90% of commercial upholstered chairs by 1981.

A major breakthrough is expected in the next two years in moulded plastic having an internal texture similar to wood, as well as external.

*Gross National Product (GNP) measures price changes in respect of goods and services currently produced. GNP is an amalgam of parts of the retail and wholesale price indices; certain earnings indices and other measures of cost increase in the construction industries and transport. It is a valuable guide to the trend in the economy generally.

4.4 ASSUMPTIONS QUANTIFIED

	Historical				Current Projections year						
	1977	1978	1979	1980	1981	1982	1983	1984	1985	1986
Gross national product*	560	589	629	676	732	747	762	777	792	815
Population, millions	53.9	54.6	55.1	55.3	55.3	55.4	55.5	55.9	60.0	60.2
Capital expenditure, £billions	1,822	2,130	2,187	2,042	2,428	3,200	3,400	3,600	3,250	3,200
Industrial production furniture index				155	163	171	180	189	198	208
Conference room furniture index		22.6	22.6	23.8	25.0	25.0	25.0	25.5	26.3	27.6

*£ billions

38

5 Objectives

The financial objectives of FCM at 1 January 1982 are to achieve:

- An annual sales growth rate of 10% up to 1986
- An annual return on sales, before tax, of 15%
- An annual return on shareholders' funds, after tax, of 35%
- New product* sales of not less than 10% of total annual sales
- No individual market contributing more than 40% of the total sales
- A national market share for the company's traditional products of not less than 10%

*A new product is one that has been on the market for less than two years.

Net sales by product line, £'000

Product line	Historical				Current year	Projections				
	1977	1978	1979	1980	1981	1982	1983	1984	1985	1986
Chairs, wooden	570	500	500	450	400	400	400	400	250	220
Chairs, wooden, upholstered	250	500	750	800	850	950	840	960	1,075	1,150
Chairs, metal, upholstered	—	—	50	250	400	450	480	540	745	950
Tables, wooden	80	100	140	150	200	220	230	250	280	310
Tables, wooden or metal	—	—	15	75	100	125	150	170	200	240
Services	—	—	25	35	50	55	100	60	160	110
Total sales	900	1,100	1,480	1,760	2,000	2,200	2,200	2,380	2,710	2,980
Gap to be filled by new products							220	280	320	340
Total sales	900	1,100	1,480	1,760	2,000	2,200	2,420	2,660	3,030	3,320

5.3 SUMMARY OF QUANTIFIED OBJECTIVES

	Historical				Current Projections						
					year						
	1977	1978	1979	1980	1981	1982	1983	1984	1985	1986
Profitability:										
Net profit, after tax, £'000	63	88	188	158	200	242	314	372	455	498
Customer satisfaction:										
Net sales, £'000	900	1,100	1,480	1,760	2,000	2,200	2,420	2,660	3,030	3,320
Market share (estimated), %					9.8	10.5	11.0	11.2	11.8	11.9
Productivity:										
Sales per employee, £	18,367	17,460	21,142	24,109	26,666	26,829	28,470	29,555	30,918	31,923
Profit before tax, £'000	210	240	355	420	440	484	560	670	800	1,000
Innovation:										
New product sales requirements, £'000	3	4	9	8	10	15	100	150	150	150
Resources:										
Stock and work-in-progress, £'000	340	350	380	460	470	470	480	485	545	595
Number of employees	49	63	70	73	75	82	85	90	98	104
Bank borrowing, £'000	160	270	285	390	395	480	626	844	904	821
Employee turnover, %	—	—	2.5	3.0	3.5	3.0	2.5	2.5	2.0	2.0

41

5.4 SUMMARY OF PROJECTED PROFIT AND LOSS ACCOUNTS AND BALANCE SHEETS

(Based on 1981 Company Plan)

	1982	1983	1984	1985	1986
Profit and loss account, £'000:					
Sales	2,200	2,420	2,660	3,030	3,320
Profit before tax	484	560	670	800	1,000
Profit after tax	242	314	372	455	498
Ratios:					
Annual sales growth (10% min.), %	10.0	10.0	10.0	13.9	9.6
Pre-tax return on sales (15% min.), %	22.0	23.1	25.2	26.4	30.1
New product sales (10% min.), %		9.1	10.5	10.6	10.2
Highest individual market (40% max.), %	43.2	34.7	36.1	35.5	34.6

	1982	*1983*	*1984*	*1985*	*1986*
Balance sheet, £'000:					
FIXED ASSETS	770	1,070	1,330	1,680	1,820
Stock	470	480	485	545	595
Debtors	370	420	470	500	550
	840	900	955	1,045	1,145
Creditors	400	400	425	450	475
NET CURRENT ASSETS	440	500	530	595	670
TOTAL NET ASSETS	1,210	1,570	1,860	2,275	2,490
Share capital	100	100	100	200	200
Retained profit*	330	544	616	871	1,169
	430	644	716	1,071	1,369
Long-term loan	300	300	300	300	300
Bank borrowing	480	626	844	904	821
CAPITAL EMPLOYED	1,210	1,570	1,860	2,275	2,490
Ratios:					
*Retained profit stated after paying dividends	100	100	200	200	200
After-tax return on shareholders' funds (35% min.), %	20.0	20.0	20.0	20.0	20.0
Gearing ratio, %	64.5	59.0	61.5	52.9	45.0

6-10 Further details

6.1 POLICIES — PROCEDURES

7.1 PROGRAMMES/ PROJECTS — KEY RESULT AREAS

The business of the company shall be conducted according to written policies, where applicable:

FCM Employment Policy
FCM Merit Review Policy
FCM Pricing Policy
FCM Social Policy

Each policy should be summarised and consideration given to necessary revisions.

(Incorporate checklist on content of policy appertaining to company.)

(As identified in Section 3.1)

Customer satisfaction (Sales Director):
Reorganise sales force

Productivity (Production Director):
Materials handling and storage project

Innovation (Sales Director):
Market research – product diversification

Resources (Finance and Production Directors):
Facilities improvement

Management development (Finance Director to co-ordinate):
Profit-planning programme

Employee attitude (Personnel Director):
Employee motivation programme

Public responsibility (Production Director):
Safety programme

[A brief description of salient features of each project or programme would be stated.]

(As identified in Section 7.1)

Facilities improvement:
  Report on land, January 1982
  Commence internal work, March 1982

Profit planning programme:
  Company plan by December 1981
  Department plans by February 1982
  Functional plans by March 1982

Reorganise sales force:
  Two (2) new Sales Managers by September
   1982

Market research – product diversification:
  Report on allied products April 1982

Management development programme:
  Supervisory follow-up, March 1982

Cost-reduction programme:
  Continuous monitoring and monthly report
   throughout 1982

Employee motivation programme:
  Training programme May and September
   1982 and plan 1983

Materials handling and storage programme:
  Reports available for action May 1982

Safety programme:
  Continuous implementation and monitoring
   with full reports quarterly

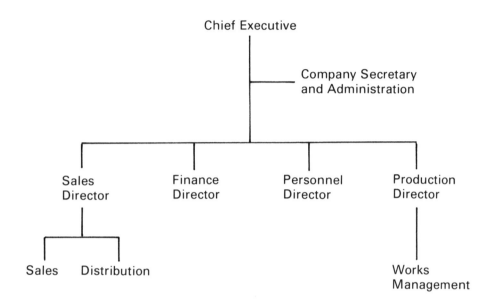

10.1 OPERATIONAL BUDGET

Major items, £'000, 1982	Year total
Net sales	2,200
Cost of sales	1,026
Gross profit	1,174
Depreciation	100
Marketing	452
Central administration	60
Interest on loan	30
Interest on other borrowing	48
Net profit	484
Taxation	242
Net profit after tax	242
Customer debts	370
Stocks and work-in-progress	470
Capital expenditure	600
Net assets	1,210
Return on net assets, %	46.5%

The above figures are to be allocated on a monthly basis and charged to departments on the basis of 'responsibility accounting'.

10.2 ACTION LIST WHEN PLAN AGREED

The agreed plan to be adopted by executive or most authoritative management body.

A detailed financial budget prepared. The first year in detail, the remaining years in outline.

The detailed budget to be analysed by function responsibility, e.g. sales, production, etc.

The budget fed into the management accounting system to ensure that recording procedures are adequate.

The accounting function consults with the heads of other functions to ensure information available is the management information required.

The planning/implementation cycle as shown on page 4 sets out the procedure.

Does the plan as prepared:

Provide a flexible posture necessary for the company's long-term survival?

Assess the vulnerability to change in competition, technological changes, new product development, etc?

Allow for the long lead time for change to be implemented?

Allow for the replacement of mature products complementing their product life?

Take account of a probable changing environment?

Indicate the most appropriate and flexible management structure?

Enable individual accountability to be discharged by identifying performance standards?

Take account of competitor's pricing policy, supply and demand of products available in market?

Take account of present and projected sales force availability of suitable recruits, training and management development?

Depend on new and revised product design taking account of customer requirements as reported by sales force?

Take account of limitations of factory space available at the existing site or in the locality?

Depend on machinery incorporating new technology – is it available and what is the lead time between order and delivery?

Lead to buy or make decisions relating to sub-component parts?

Quantify the benefits of subcontracting complete product ranges?

Necessitate increase in employees engaged in production? Is a suitable source available? What training facilities and costs are envisaged?

Permit maximum use of distribution facilities against probable customer growth and location?

Relate to the management information system and control procedures?

Rely on both financial data and non-financial data?

Indicate a requirement for information to flow vertically as well as horizontally?

Fall within the financial resources of the company?

Will the banks support the projected financial requirements?

Can the existing owners undertake to increase the capital in 1981? Are the returns adequate?

What are the top-side and bottom-side risks of a profit range?

Does the accounting and administration function require strengthening?

Adequately recognise the company's objectives; is a change in the objectives necessary?

Form the basis for the development of an additional plan?

How to plan and control business

The recognition of a problem is the start of its solution. More often than not the fact that the problem exists escapes notice unless the planning and the monitoring systems can relate to each other.

Short-term planning is introduced into the management information system by means of budgetary control – the yardstick of performance and achievement.

The argument is often advanced that to plan is to deploy costly management time in esoteric thinking with little probability of payback. In reality, survival of the enterprise may depend on comparing performance against effective yardsticks and taking the appropriate corrective action.

The management of *Leisure Sound Limited*, the following example, were disappointed in their achievements, but no information was available within the company by which their disappointment could be measured. There was no plan, hence no budget, therefore no direction – at least the problem was recognised. The fact that remedial reorganisation had timely recognition was the catalyst for future advancement.

The only practical and sensible course of action was followed. Each facet of the company was identified and examined against soundly based, accepted management principles. There is no right or wrong way to structure or control an activity. The course which remedial action will take depends on each circumstance and the goals set.

The costs involved in running an efficient enterprise are probably only marginally greater than those normally required within the inefficient enterprise. It is the manner in which costs are incurred and the effectiveness of the result which matters.

The initial aspects of *Leisure Sound's* plan consisted of consideration in the following main areas:

Management
Marketing
Production
Accounting

together with the Personnel function – the custodian of the people resource embracing these four functional areas.

The use of checklists ensured that no vital question or area of enquiry was overlooked. Resources – people, raw material, accommodation and money – were allocated to individuals on the basis of accountability. Everyone in the company became responsible to someone for something.

The plans were translated into budgets which became a vital part of the management system. The individuals comprising the company were thereby motivated along a predetermined route.

Since progress is evolutionary, the lessons learned in the first year of the reorganisation would be built into the planning checklists for the following and subsequent years and management goals would become progressively more demanding. Most enterprises thrive on discipline.

Leisure Sound Limited

The history of a company that did not achieve expectations, analysed deficiencies and instituted remedial action

Contents of Unit 2

6   Monitoring actual performance

7   Management control information

8 Management information – monthly and quarterly

9 Summarised management control information

10 Results for 1982

1 Company background

The company was formed in 1975.

Acquired two small but expanding businesses: one manufacturing high-quality loudspeakers, the other a compact radio, amplifier and turntable unit.

The original proprietors remained with the company until 1978.

The management team then recruited is with the company at the present time.

The capital of the company is owned by members of the board of directors.

The style of management until the end of 1981 was such that:
Decision-taking was unco-ordinated.
Members of the team invariably took individual decisions.
These decisions affected either the company as a whole or activities within the factory.

No one individual had established lines of authority or responsibility.

The company decided that it should concentrate its marketing (because of the competitive market and consequent high-risk area) on complete 'Music Systems' (consisting of an FM/AM stereo tuner; stereo amplifier, turntable and two loudspeakers) all of high quality.

That where a demand existed, individual units of the system should be sold.

In order to control the quality, products should be manufactured or assembled or both.

The high reproductive quality of the product assures continued growth of the company.

The geographical area of growth was restricted.

1.3 FACTORY

1.4 MANAGEMENT INFORMATION SYSTEM

The factory is modern but production and assembly facilities have grown piecemeal to meet market demand.

The operations undertaken in the factory are:
1 Manufacture of wooden loudspeaker cabinets.
2 Assembly of loudspeaker units.
3 Assembly of cabinet with unit.
4 Assembly of combined tuner/amplifier and turntable units.
5 Packing of the latter with twin loudspeaker cabinets to form a 'Music System'.

The factory also incorporates offices and garage accommodation.

A simple form of management accounting system is in operation, mainly consisting of monthly sales information and, at year end (31 December), a profit and loss account and balance sheet.

Elementary controls exist regarding the collection and payment of cash from customers and to creditors.

The directors were very distressed to have established in late December the probable results for the company's financial year to 31 December 1981, given the level of activity, skill and hours worked by all senior company employees.

To summarise:

1 The profit before tax at £145,000 would fall short of expectation by £30,000 (or 17.1% of £175,000, the profit expectation).
2 The return on year-end net assets excluding borrowings would be only 24%, against the predetermined necessary level of 40.0%.
3 The overdraft would be higher than at the end of the 1980 year by £24,000 and would probably be at a level of £80,000.

The probability had to be accepted that the company's bank would not advance further facilities.

The directors' expectations for 1981 were based on the increasing trend of activity for the year to 31 December 1980 and, had this continued together with effective control of expenditure and levels of production, the expected results would have been capable of achievement.

In anticipation of a more rewarding potential, additional capital amounting to £66,000 had been introduced at the beginning of the 1981 trading year.

The actual results for the year ended 31 December 1981 are shown on the profit and loss account and balance sheet below along with those for 1980.

Leisure Sound: Profit and loss account for year ended 31 December

	1981 actual, £'000	1980 actual, £'000
Sales	1,800	1,550
Stock at 1 January 1981	200	150
Purchases	711	640
	911	790
Deduct: stock at 31 December 1981	236	200
Cost of materials	675	590
Overheads and other expenditure	940	795
Depreciation	40	25
Total cost of sales	1,655	1,410
Profit before tax	145	140
Taxation	70	65
Profit after tax	75	75
Dividend	45	40
Retained and added to reserves	30	35

Leisure Sound: Net assets at 31 December

	1981 actual, £'000	1980 actual, £'000
Fixed assets		
Goodwill	120	120
Plant and machinery	270	180
Furniture and fittings	40	30
Motor vehicles	80	60
	510	390
Net current assets		
Stock	236	220
Trade debtors	220	180
Current assets	456	400
Trade creditors	190	164
Bank overdraft	80	56
Taxation	110	80
Dividend	40	40
Current liabilities	420	340
Net current assets	36	60
Net assets	546	450
Capital employed		
Share capital	400	334
Reserves	36	1
Retained profit	30	35
	66	36
Shareholders' funds	466	370
Long-term loan	80	80
Capital employed	546	450

2 The background to a plan

The directors decided that the company's
objectives should be established as the basis of
a plan which should cover the following areas:

2.1 MANAGEMENT

Job responsibility
Effectiveness
Accountability

2.3 PRODUCTION

Facilities
Capacity
Utilisation and break-even point
Workforce availability
Probable expansion requirement

2.2 MARKETING

Customer sector
Competition
Trend of industry; technological and allied
  developments
New products development
Customer demand
Design
Manufacturing capability

2.4 ACCOUNTING

Minimum return criteria
Costing and control information
Available finance and cash flow
Monitoring of the results

3 The analysis

Examining the overall trading and financial position, the directors set down for answer a few basic questions relating to the main areas of their business, namely:

Management
Products
Manufacturing
Marketing
Personnel
Finance and accounting

Is the management structure of the company adequate?

Is the company capable of absorbing change?

Is it flexible in a constantly changing environment?

Are the skills available sufficient and used in the most effective manner?

What is the age distribution of the present management team?

Are any gaps apparent?

3.3 PRODUCTS CHECKLIST

Are the products as good as the management think?

Are changes apparent in customer trends or needs?

Does the quality of the product improve at the same rate as, for example, records or tapes?

Is styling an important feature to customer appeal?

Is sufficient resource given to research and development?

Is monitoring competition important?

3.4 MANUFACTURING CHECKLIST

What is the state and condition of the plant and equipment?

Is the factory layout efficient and economical?

Is the plant sufficiently flexible?

Are quality control facilities up to acceptable requirements?

What effort is associated with the examination of new technology?

3.5 MARKETING CHECKLIST

Is the sales force of the appropriate quantity and quality?

What relevance is price?

What market researching is regularly undertaken?

Which advertising and sales promotion is involved?

Are the present channels of distribution adequate?

3.6 PERSONNEL CHECKLIST

Is the salary and wage structure adequate in changing labour market?

Are social responsibilities important?

Is unionisation a problem now or in the future?

Are employees motivated to maximum efficiency?

Can employees be educated or trained for the new requirements?

Would a system of allocating responsibility through personal objectives require measurement and would it stimulate motivation and efficiency?

What is the minimum acceptable level of profit and return on net assets?

How can this be achieved? More sales? Lower cost with limited assets or a mix of these?

Is the present information system adequate?

Do efficient controls exist throughout the company?

Is a system of budgetary control helpful or essential?

Where are future sources of funds to be generated and how much will be required?

4 The plan

4.1 THE PLANNING PROCESS

The directors examined each function on the bases of strengths and weaknesses. An example of the type of plan then produced from an amalgamation of their total input is shown in the corporate planning model (see Unit 1, p. 4).

As a first attempt certain standards were set for the planning process.

The plan must,
1   Be simple and concentrate on essentials.
2   Be understood by all senior management.
3   Lead to conclusions and objectives.
4   Be moderately accurate; the temptation for pedantic accuracy must be avoided.
5   State fairly and objectively strengths and weaknesses. Strengths must be strengthened and weaknesses must be eliminated.
6   Not lead to change for change's sake.
7   Prepare the company and its management for action.
8   Provide a fuller knowledge of the company and its potential.
9   Be the commitment of management.
10 Result in action.
11 Be capable of being monitored.

4.2 THE OBJECTIVES

The directors having considered the company plan in detail, the following main objectives were established for 1982.

Personnel:

An effective management structure will be established to fit individuals to the task to be performed.

The individuals concerned will have their tasks specified and be responsible for operating within the limits of their authority.

An effective system of monitoring the performance of the task against an agreed budget will be developed.

Financial:

Sales must grow at a rate of 22% from the 1981 level.

Profit before tax must be not less than £260,000.

The profit margin on sales should be not less than 11.5%.

The return on net assets, measured at December 1982, to be not less than 40%.

A budgetary control system to be introduced from 1 January 1982.

5 The implementation of the plan

5.1 MANAGEMENT STRUCTURE

The analysis of the situation identified the tasks to be performed against which it was possible to experiment with the design of the management structure. This structure had to take into account both the style by which the company would be managed, i.e. rigid, flexible, established limits of authority, etc., and the responsibilities to be covered.

Section 5.1.1. describes the basic structure which was further expanded to show the inter-relationship of the subsidiary responsibilities as in Section 5.1.2.

The details included in the job specification for each of the senior management team are shown in Sections 5.1.4 to 5.1.9.

5.1.1 Outline management structure

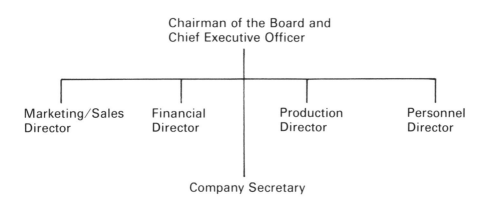

The Company Secretary while acting as Secretary to the Board is additionally the executive responsible for administration.

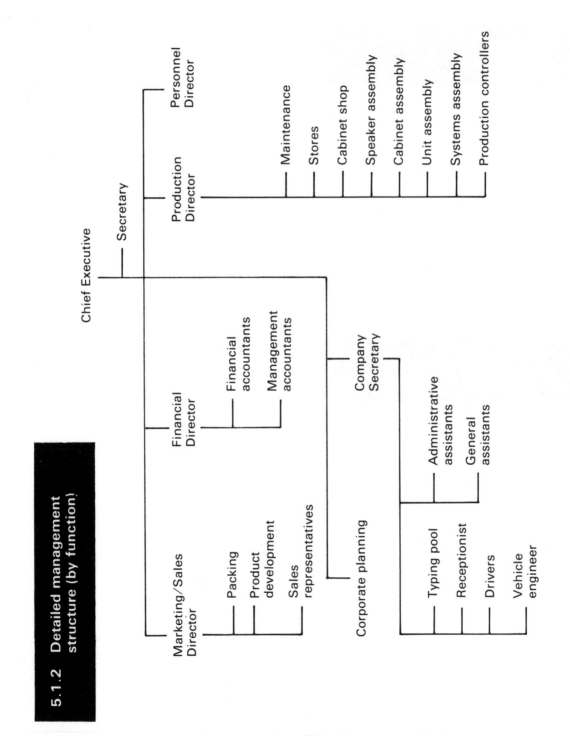

5.1.2 Detailed management structure (by function)

Chief Executive

Secretary

Marketing/Sales Director
- Packing
- Product development
- Sales representatives

Financial Director
- Financial accountants
- Management accountants

Production Director
- Maintenance
- Stores
- Cabinet shop
- Speaker assembly
- Cabinet assembly
- Unit assembly
- Systems assembly
- Production controllers

Personnel Director

Corporate planning

Company Secretary
- Administrative assistants
- General assistants
- Typing pool
- Receptionist
- Drivers
- Vehicle engineer

5.1.3 Detailed job descriptions: introduction

5.1.4 Job description: chief executive

The following job descriptions are indicative only and relate to the structure of and the example job requirements in Leisure Sound. The basis can apply to most situations and should be extended to show:

1   To whom the job holder is responsible.
2   Those subordinates who are directly responsible to the job holder.

A job specification checklist should include

a   The job title of the individual to whom the job holder reports.
b   The job titles of each of the individuals reporting directly to the job holder.
c   A summary for each immediate sub-ordinate of the overall purpose of the job and the main functions or activities which are carried out or for which responsibility attaches.
d   Wherever possible, quantitative data should be obtained on the scale of the activities of each subordinate or the section controlled by the subordinate.
e   Details of the organisation structure under each subordinate, including the number and types of staff they supervise.

Ideally the job specification should indicate freedoms such as
    to act within a given policy
    formulate own targets
    changing the organisation structure of your department
    promotion
    salary increases
    job regrading
    discipline
    level of control information
    limits and method of expenditure

Leisure Sound Limited: Chief Executive

Job purpose:

Development of the company's character and reputation.

Financial performance and growth of the company.

Perpetuation and self-renewal of the company.

Leadership of the senior executives.

Monitoring of all standards set and job achievements.

Specific duties:

Determining the objectives of the company with the board of directors and developing plans to achieve these.

Formulating policy requirements.

Determining the basic organisational structure and ensuring that job holders are skilled to discharge their accountabilities.

Setting standards and the surveillance of performance and morale.

Establishing corporate priorities and the allocation of resources.

Maintaining effective external relationships.

Developing a succession plan.

5.1.5 Job description: marketing director

Leisure Sound Limited: Marketing Director

Job purpose:

Product planning: both updating existing models and identifying new models with adequate economic return.

Designing a pricing policy which will meet the company's financial criteria and compete with competitive products.

Achieve market penetration as laid down in the objectives or financial strategy.

Develop an economic sales force to achieve above.

Specific duties:

In conjunction with the personnel function, identify the company's sales force requirement and develop, recruit and establish a sales force with a commensurate remuneration package where targets are achieved.

Set standards for sales force based on factory capacities and production schedules.

Decide upon the requirement of a salary structure and institute with assistance from the personnel function. Establish overall costs of marketing/sales department and procedure for monitoring.

Develop sales promotion campaigns, product planning and innovation, product diversification and packaging with such market research as necessary.

Design display material with promotion ideas; along with advertising in accordance with the agreed advertising budget. Ensure that total public relations strategy is related to product advertising.

Establish feedback pattern for reporting of competitive trends and new or revised products, in particular, of revised styling.

Constantly review competition trends against company's policy regarding mail order wholesale and other distribution channels.

Ensure that quality control is effective and that after sales service is adequate.

Establishing with finance function effective Sales Ledger, Invoicing, Credit Control and bad debt recovery procedures with feedback on customers through Sales Force.

Leisure Sound Limited: Production Director

Job Purpose:

Ensure efficient machine utilisation achieves maximum production capacity.

Achieve specified delivery times with effective quality control.

Raw material and bought-in parts are the most economical for the purpose required and the source of supply is reviewed constantly.

Review regularly all technological development in production and assembly processes.

Specific duties:

Maintain efficient production loading by establishing trained supervisory and other workforce with an effective control system.

Examine factory layout to take account of changing production requirements and re-budget as necessary.

Keep all buying procedures under review to ensure stock control levels compatible with production schedules and lead times with minimum investment in stock.

Review quality and terms of suppliers' products.

Set production standards and review these as product schedules are altered to accommodate sales requirements. Review regularly efficiency and cost control procedures.

Establish worker participation in management of department through 'quality circles' and the like.

Establish training routines and aim to reduce labour turnover by observance of wage rates and those paid locally.

Define quality control requirements and liaise with marketing department to ensure elimination of customer complaints.

Relentlessly pursue late delivery against promised dates and revise procedures to eliminate delays.

Define machine and equipment maintenance schedules and develop procedure to ensure repairs are effective to avoid disruption to production.

Observe health and safety procedures.

Liaise with finance function to ensure management information and departmental accounts are understood and acted upon.

Leisure Sound Limited: Personnel Director

Job purpose:

Establish an effective remuneration structure.

Identify training needs of the company and establish a training programme for all levels of management.

Ensure that management development is compatible with the corporate manpower plan.

Establish a data recording system to encapsulate information to achieve the above.

Specific duties:

Manage and control the minimum establishment and cost to achieve the following requirements and to review these from time to time.

Establish with functional colleagues an effective and challenging system for recruitment and monitor the effectiveness of such systems.

Identify the training needs of the company's workforce and establish training systems both internally and externally as necessary.

Advise executive colleagues on most effective management structure and review and make recommendations as necessary.

Establish a salary and remuneration structure for the company's needs and ensure that this structure is kept in line with economic conditions and remuneration trends within the appropriate industry and as far as possible in line with those adopted by competitive organisations.

Maintain adequate personnel records.

Prepare and input to manpower plans within the company's corporate planning timetable and review total manpower planning requirements.

Prepare succession plans within an acceptable planning horizon to take account of recruitment and training or retraining as necessary, development of existing staff with the required performance review procedures.

Establish termination and redundancy policies.

Establish effective labour/union relations.

Ensure that the provisions and requirements of health and safety legislation are observed.

Maintain a pension policy compatible with company's profitability and ensure advantage is taken of changing legislation where benefits could accrue to both company and employees.

Establish effective communication systems.

Leisure Sound Limited: Financial Director

Job purpose:

The development of broad financial strategies.

The establishment of strict financial disciplines on all aspects of the company's affairs.

The establishment and operation of realistic financial control and management information systems.

The establishment of common accounting practices throughout the company.

Advising the board on the financial effects of policies and programmes and projects requiring board authority.

Raising finance as necessary.

Ensuring the maximum benefits, under current tax legislation.

Specific duties:

Financial control. In conjunction with other senior management, design and develop an integrated control and management information system to cover all facets of the company's operation.

Implement an effective cost accounting and information system.

Supervise the preparation of periodic reports on the company's performance against operating budgets and standards.

Co-ordinate preparation and consolidation of the annual profit plans, budgets and forecasts.

Ensure that overheads are monitored against budget.

Accounting. Supervise the development of the systems and procedures.

Ensure that the company complies with its statutory obligations.

Liaise with the group's auditors.

Formulate finance policies and the capital structure of the company.

Manage and advise on the use of working capital.

Review all capital expenditure proposals, carrying out further investigations where necessary.

Supervise company's taxation policy.

Advise the executive committee on economic developments likely to influence the company.

Leisure Sound Limited: Company Secretary

Job purpose:

Assist the board of the company to effectively discharge its duties.

Provide a legal advisory service for the company and ensure that such expertise as required is readily available.

Attend to the legal requirements relating to property, trade marks and patents and ensure protection of the company's assets.

Control the company's distribution vehicles to provide a cost-effective service.

Specific duties:

Ensuring, on behalf of the board, that the company's legal responsibilities under the Companies Acts and other statutes and by-laws are fulfilled.

Preparing agenda and other documents for meetings of the board and the company.

Ensuring that the business of formal meetings is recorded correctly.

That obligations under leases of property are observed and efficiently discharged.

Ensure that the company is adequately covered by insurance and deal with all insurance matters which arise.

To retain such records of the company's patents, trade-marks and other trade agreements.

To provide or obtain such specialised legal advice or services which may be required by the company or its senior executives.

Appraise the communication network.

Take responsibility for the motor vehicle fleet, its effective maintenance and replacement and to ensure that all statutory requirements are fulfilled.

Control the central administration staff and consider costs of services against the services which must be provided. Ensure that the standard of these services are maintained at a high level.

Liaise with all functional departments in the administration of pension funds and other general matters affecting the company and its staff.

5.2.1 Factory layout checklist

The factory consists of 100,000 sq. ft. and is of modern construction with facilities for the repair and maintenance of vehicles.

The company's operations lend themselves to five self-contained units of production or assembly.

Efficiency is maintained by ease of storage of raw materials, components and finished stock and effective methods of transfer of completed units from one area to the next.

In arriving at the final layout as shown in Section 5.2.3 the following was used as a checklist:

Is the factory and its administrative facilities suitable for the requirements of the company plan?

How much extra space is available now, if any, and when will this be fully utilised?

If there is extra space can this be used profitably in the short term?

Can raw material and component stocks be contained within allocated areas at maximum stock levels?

Can production facilities be set out easily to accommodate the manufacture and assembly processes?

Can production demarcation lines be maintained effectively?

Is the factory economic in the use of energy?

Are any local authority or other planning requirements likely to interfere or disrupt factory utilisation?

Are the storage facilities capable of holding maximum stock without undue bottlenecks and possible damage?

Can efficient flow lines be maintained throughout the factory and from store to despatch?

Is it intended to maintain own transport and are facilities available for major overhauls?

What facilities are available locally as extra storage space and can this be obtained quickly?

Are loading bays and despatch points effective?

Is easy access to the factory site possible?

The area attributed to each operation (either administrative, production or marketing) was measured, the following being an approximate indication of the area involved and the executive responsible.

	Area, ft^2
Administration:	
Executive	2,500
Company Secretary (of which Transport 25,000 ft^2)	35,000
Personnel	2,500
Finance and accounting	5,000
Corporate development	1,250
Production:	
Cabinet shop manager	10,000
Speaker assembly manager	7,500
Cabinet assembly manager	7,500
Unit assembly manager	12,500
System assembly manager	7,500
	45,000 45,000
Marketing:	
General	7,500
Packing	1,250
	8,750 8,750
	100,000

This analysis forms the basis of cost allocation for expenditure relating to rent and rates as shown in Section 5.4.3.

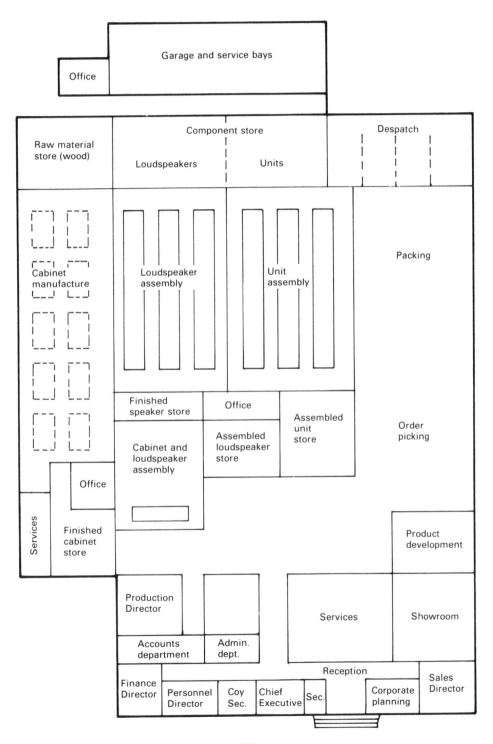

77

5.3 DETAILED MANAGEMENT STRUCTURE

The management structure shown in Section 5.1.1. and expanded to show functional responsibilities in Section 5.1.2 was further detailed as in Section 5.3.1 to staff and employee numbers and associated remuneration costs.

The detail incorporated within the structure is essentially for the apportionment of expenditure to cost centres in accordance with agreed budgetary control procedures, details of which follow in Section 5.3.1.

It would be unusual to show such detail on a structure diagram which was available generally for all levels of management.

The remunerations shown in Section 5.3.1 are for illustrative purposes only and bear no relationship to actual scales of remuneration paid in the marketplace for similar job responsibilities to those listed in Sections 5.1.4 to 5.1.9.

5.3.1 Detailed management structure by staff members and remuneration

Chief Executive (£12,000)

Secretary (£3000)

Personnel Director (£7000)

Production Director (£8000)
- Maintenance (2 at £4000)
- Stores (1 at £3000)
- Cabinet shop (10 at £25,000)
- Speaker assembly (8 at £15,000)
- Cabinet assembly (7 at £15,000)
- Unit assembly (3 at £10,000)
- Systems assembly (2 at £5000)
- Production controllers (5 at £10,000)

Financial Director (£10,000)
- Financial accountants (2 at £6000)
- Management accountants (3 at £6000)

Company Secretary (£7000)
- Administrative assistants (3 at £8000)
- General assistants (3 at £5000)

Marketing/Sales Director (£10,000)
- Packing (3 at £9000)
- Sales representatives (3 at £12,000)
- Production development (2 at £6000)

Corporate planning (£6000)
- Typing Pool (3 at £9000)
- Receptionist (1 at £2000)
- Drivers (3 at £9000)
- Vehicle engineer (£3000)

Total staff = 73

Total payroll = £225,000

79

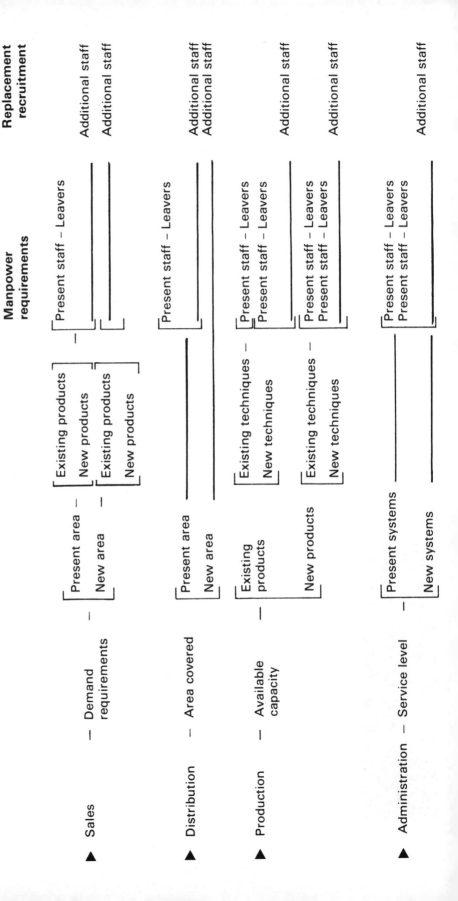

5.3.2 Elements of a manpower plan

Manpower requirements

Replacement recruitment

▲ Sales — Demand requirements

Present area —
- Existing products
- New products

Present staff – Leavers

New area —
- Existing products
- New products

Present staff – Leavers → Additional staff
Additional staff

▲ Distribution — Area covered

Present area

New area

Present staff – Leavers

Additional staff
Additional staff

▲ Production — Available capacity

Existing products —
- Existing techniques
- New techniques

Present staff – Leavers
Present staff – Leavers

Additional staff

New products —
- Existing techniques
- New techniques

Present staff – Leavers
Present staff – Leavers

Additional staff

▲ Administration — Service level

Present systems

New systems

Present staff – Leavers
Present staff – Leavers

Additional staff

Having established the

● Management structure by areas of responsibility (Section 5.1.2)

● Factory layout (Section 5.2.3)

● Total establishment within these areas and associated employment costs (Section 5.3.1)

there remained to be prepared

● An estimate of the costs to be incurred during 1982

● An allocation of these costs to 'cost centres' in line with individual responsibility and the operation under the executives' control

● A summary of that expenditure (Section 5.4.1)

Leisure Sound Limited

List of probable expenditure for the year to 31 December 1982

Employment costs		250,000
Salaries	225,000	
Pensions	14,000	
Nat. Ins.	11,000	
Energy		26,000
Advertising		15,000
Telephone		10,000
Insurance		7,000
Travelling		5,000
Rent		400,000
Rates		228,000
General		4,000
Administration		5,000
Bank interest		10,000
		£960,000
Depreciation		£65,000
Total		£1,025,000

81

The directors have, using the basis for cost apportionment in Section 5.4.3, allocated to the pre-determined cost centres the total estimated cost of £1,025,000 for the year to 31 December 1982.

● Part of these costs are 'controllable', i.e. within the control of the executives responsible and amount to £310,000, together with the charge for depreciation of £65,000, the remainder amounting to £375,000.

● Some costs cannot be directly apportioned on an 'accountability' basis and are therefore spread over the cost centres on the basis listed in Section 5.4.3. The direct non-controllable costs amount to £650,000.

The total estimated costs of £1,025,000, including depreciation of £65,000 as shown in Section 5.4.1, are not allocated to cost centres as follows:

Cost centre		Executive responsible
Executive	34,000	Chief Executive
Administration	96,500	Company Secretary
Personnel	27,000	Personnel Director
Secretarial	19,000	Company Secretary
Finance and Accounting	60,000	Financial Director
Corporate development	14,500	Chief Executive
Production control and maintenance	39,500	Production Director
Cabinet shop	113,500	Production Director
Speaker assembly	73,500	Production Director
Cabinet assembly	73,000	Production Director
Unit assembly	100,500	Production Director
System assembly	61,500	Production Director
Marketing, despatch and sales	109,000	Sales and Marketing Director
Transport, delivery and storage	203,500	Company Secretary
	£1,025,000	

The following basis was used for the allocation of expenditure to the cost centres:

Non-controllable expenditure

Rent:	Area utilised
Rates:	Area utilised
Insurance:	Balance of insurance costs not allocated to specific departments or activities allocated on basis of area.
General:	Mix of employees, departmental expenditure and selling or transfer value of production.
Administration:	As for 'General'.
Bank interest:	Average capital invested in fixed and circulating assets.
Depreciation:	Related to the written-down value of assets used.

Controllable expenditure

Employment costs:

Salaries and wages:	Numbers of employees allocated to executive, administration and production.
Pensions:	Company's contribution on an individual basis relative to gross pay.
Nat. Ins.:	Employees.

Energy:	Estimated basis after allowing for direct production and assembly costs and based upon floor area or cubic area affected.
Advertising:	Product advertised.
Telephone:	Direct costs related to raw materials or component purchase and machine upkeep and repairs.
Insurance:	Valuation of property allocated by area used. Plant and stock by value. Total payroll dependent upon risk insured.
Travelling:	Actual incurred.

Cost control checklist

Does the cost control system have the active backing of top management?

Do controls conform to the organisation structures?

Is the system seen as being an essential part of the company's management process?

Are responsible individuals aware of the need to plan their activities?

Do those individuals charged with various costs agree the reasonableness of these costs?

Are cost controls established according to the nature of the tasks?

Do all who require it receive effective cost information?

83

Do individuals who are held accountable play a constructive role in setting cost levels?

Is cost control information geared to the requirements of individuals responsible?

Is the costing system adequate in general terms?

Do control reports cover both financial and related causal factors? If not, should they?

Are cost control requirements and reports discussed with recipients?

Does the basis of measuring desired performance reflect those aspects of output and input that are important?

Is the principle of management by exception followed?

Are results measured in accordance with the same units of measure in which the standards are set?

Do recipients of control information know how to extract the most essential facts?

Are controls flexible and economical in operation?

Are deviations reported rapidly?

Do controls help to explain variances and to indicate the corrective action that is required?

Are control reports brief, simple to read, and relevant?

Are actions taken on the basis of these reports?

Are control reports used to indicate relative efficiencies?

Do all employees understand the cost implications of their work?

Do all employees have cost targets?

Do the benefits of the cost control system outweigh its costs?

Are unnecessary reports eliminated, and are new ones introduced only when clearly needed?

Is the control system revised each time an organisational change takes place?

Do good relations exist between the accounting function and line management?

Essentially there are four distinct but inter-related sections relating to the preparation of a budget and its quantification:

1 The selling function with a projection of sales trends and the associated cost of raw material, manufacture and assembly.
2 The establishment of overhead and general administration costs.
3 Based mainly on the first, the requirement for additional capital investment in plant, stock and work-in-progress and in the case of sales on credit, debtors.
4 The incidence of timing on both income and expenditure resulting in the ascertain-.ment of the internal cashflow and the possible peaks and troughs within the budget period.

Of the above, the establishment of overhead and general administration costs is probably the area whereby greatest accuracy can be obtained because,

● Cost budgets are built mainly on past trends of known expenditure.
● Cost budgets are prepared after strategic decisions have to be taken, e.g. to extend a section of factory or to hire or purchase another delivery vehicle each with associated known costs.
● Cost budgets contain 'blocks' of fixed expenditure unaffected by changes in volume sales.

Given the above, there still remains the quantification of the effects of inflation and general cost increases over which the enterprise has little, if any, control and which must be built into the budgets. This is an area demanding the highest management judgement – since cost escalation is the result of many external and economic factors, e.g. the strength of the national currency and the cost of imported fuel. Past trends of cost escalation over a period of years will be helpful but can only be applied to budget costs after considering other available information over these trends from government or reliable trade sources.

Leisure Sound Ltd
Budget expenditure by cost centre: year to 31 December 1982

Figures in £	Total	Administration				
		Executive	Admin.	Personnel	Secretarial	Finance & accounting
(a) Controllable costs*						
Salaries and wages	225,000	12,000	7,000	7,000		10,000
(as per management		3,000	9,000			12,000
structure)			8,000			
			5,000			
			2,000			
Pension	14,000	1,000	1,000	1,000		1,000
National Insurance	11,000	500	1,500	1,000		1,000
Total employment costs	250,000	16,500	33,500	9,000		24,000
Energy	26,000	500	1,000	1,000	1,000	1,500
Advertising	15,000					
Telephone	10,000	500	3,000	500	1,000	1,000
Insurance	4,000		500			500
Travelling	5,000	500	1,500	500	500	
	310,000	18,000	39,500	11,000	2,500	27,000
(b) Non-controllable costs						
Rent	400,000	10,000	30,000	10,000	10,000	20,000
Rates	228,000	6,000	18,000	6,000	6,000	7,000
Insurance	3,000		3,000			
General	4,000		3,000			
Administration	5,000		3,000	500	500	1,000
Bank interest	10,000					
	650,000	16,000	57,000	16,500	16,500	28,000
Summary:						
(a) Controllable costs	310,000	18,000	39,500	11,000	2,500	27,000
(b) Non-controllable costs	650,000	16,000	57,000	16,500	16,500	28,000
	960,000	34,000	96,500	27,500	19,000	55,000
Depreciation	65,000					5,000
	1,025,000	34,000	96,500	27,500	19,000	60,000

*That is, under manager's control.

Corporate development	Production control & maintenance	Production					Marketing, sales & despatch	Transport delivery & storage
		Cabinet shop	Speaker assembly	Cabinet assembly	Unit assembly	System assembly		
6,000	8,000	25,000	15,000	15,000	10,000	5,000	10,000	3,000
	4,000	2,000	2,000	2,000	2,000	2,000	6,000	9,000
	3,000						12,000	
							9,000	
	1,000	1,000	1,500	1,500	1,500		500	3,000
500	1,500	1,500	500	1,000	500	500	500	500
6,500	17,500	29,500	19,000	19,500	14,000	7,500	38,000	15,500
		6,000	3,000	2,000	3,000	2,000	1,000	4,000
							15,000	
							4,000	
	1,000	1,000						1,000
							2,000	
6,500	18,500	36,500	22,000	21,500	17,000	9,500	60,000	20,500
5,000	5,000	40,000	30,000	30,000	50,000	30,000	30,000	100,000
3,000	3,000	18,000	18,000	18,000	30,000	18,000	18,000	59,000
	1,000							
		2,000	1,000	1,000	1,000	1,000	1,000	3,000
8,000	9,000	60,000	49,000	49,000	81,000	49,000	49,000	162,000
6,500	18,500	36,500	22,000	21,500	17,000	9,500	60,000	20,500
8,000	9,000	60,000	49,000	49,000	81,000	49,000	49,000	162,000
14,500	27,500	96,500	71,000	70,500	98,000	58,500	109,000	182,500
	12,000	17,000	2,500	2,500	2,500	2,500		21,000
14,500	39,500	113,500	73,500	73,000	100,500	61,000	109,000	203,500

Are individuals' responsibilities clearly defined?

Is the assigned authority in line with delegated responsibility in all cases?

Is delegation properly carried out?

Is the organisation chart current, adequately detailed, and available to all staff?

Could any organisational grouping be re-organised to reduce costs or improve effectiveness?

Are objectives – both corporate and departmental – established and communicated?

Are key assignments rotated? Should they be; and, if so, can they be?

Is management succession planned?

Are responsibilities divided in such a way as to permit a budgetary measurement of individual effectiveness?

Are all responsible individuals called upon to explain variances in their areas? Are follow-up actions checked?

Is every necessary function unambiguously assigned to a responsibility centre?

Are responsibilities specific and understood?

Is there any overlapping of responsibilities?

Does each individual within the organisation have one – and only one – boss?

Does an adequate coding system exist so that all cost items can readily be recorded in their proper account?

Does the chart of accounts accurately represent the organisational structure as it is rather than as it perhaps should be? Does the management information system reflect the structure?

Are all items of expense recorded in accordance with the lowest level or area of operations to which they can be directly related?

Are all needless allocations and apportionments avoided?

Are all changes in responsibilities made with a clear understanding of their impact on the part of all concerned?

Are all cases of promotion, salary increases, and disciplinary action approved by the immediate superior of the individual?

Do all disputes over questions relating to authority and responsibility receive prompt and careful consideration?

Are accurate standards set for each measureable and controllable cost element?

Are all costs clearly split into their controllable and uncontrollable categories (bearing in mind the level of authority and the time span)?

Is cost-consciousness encouraged throughout the organisation?

Do cost controls correspond with areas of organisational responsibility?

Is the performance of each responsible individual regularly measured, monitored and reported?

Are the plans/standards used in performance measurement adequate and sufficiently accurate?

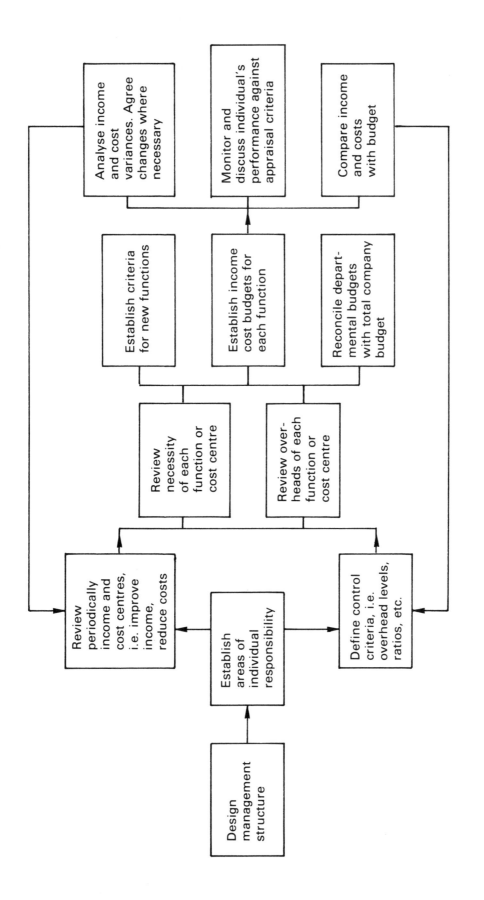

Can it be eliminated without much harm to the results?

Does it cost more than it is worth?

Can it be reduced in scope and cost?

Does it do more than is required?

Can it be done more cheaply another way?

Can it be done more cheaply by someone else?

Is there an alternative service from outside which is adequate but cheaper?

Can the service or expenses supporting the operation be reduced?

On a management judgement basis, can the operation be sensibly considered to provide its full share of overhead and net profit contribution?

How does it affect other costs in the business?

If you were to start the business again would you include it?

Using the available resources, what income can be expected from sales of the company's products?

Can the company create a demand for its products or merely satisfy an existing demand?

Has effective market research been carried out?

The Sales Director, who is responsible for the preparation of the sales income, will use the checklist in Section 5.5.1.

Is the basic concept and specification of the product acceptable to the market for which it is produced?

Is the price/performance ratio acceptable?

Are developments scheduled for existing products? Will these take the product beyond specification of competitors' products?

Will serious loss of market share arise before innovations can be incorporated and tested?

Can the competitive situations be monitored by existing sales price?

What criteria will the sales force use to ensure consistancy in reporting?

Are there strong allegances or emotional attachments within the company for existing products?

Are price wars envisaged with financially stronger competitors?

What are the cut-off points in a price war situation in order not to damage the viability of the company?

Do the marketing policies fit the corporate objectives or is it the other way around?

Are product cycles identifiable and is any of the product range vulnerable to decline?

Is there an optimum of product sales to maximise profitability?

Data requirement for marketing plan

General:

How does marketing research expenditure compare with competitors?

How effective is it?

Has the firm effective information sources?

What data is available?

What methods of marketing research have been found to be effective?

How can product intelligence be obtained?

Are independent agencies preferred to firm's own research?

Market:

Total size of market
Rate of change of size
Factors affecting changes
Number of competitors
Competitors' market share
Competitors' change in market size
Competitors' sales organisation structure
Competitors' strengths and weaknesses in
    pricing policy
Forecasts of market conditions
Seasonal/cyclical market fluctuations
Market potential (new and existing)
User characteristics/attitudes/opinions
Potential customers – kind, number and
    location
Product uses
Customers' product selection criteria, e.g. per-
    formance, size, shape, service
Sources of customer dissatisfaction
Competitive position of company products
Promotional activities
Distribution methods

New product development

What market share can be expected if company continues on present course?

How will customers' requirements and habits change?

91

What new markets are suitable?

What will be their sales potential?

When will this potential be reached?

What will need to be done – development; production; sales?

What resources will be needed, e.g. manpower?

Will financial resources be sufficient?

Will specialists be needed?

What will profit margin be?

Can we obtain an adequate market share?

How fast will the market grow?

How is the demand divided – Government/industrial/military/private?

What future market share can be expected if the products are modernised?

How will sales increase if product range is extended?

Can the sales effort be intensified and what effect will this have?

Consideration given to the above – the expected income from sales for 1982 is anticipated to be £2,200,000 as shown in Section 5.5.2.

Potential failure areas

Failing to place responsibility at a sufficiently high level

Failing to establish a real unanimity of objectives

Setting unrealistic criteria in a competitive sellers' market

Searching only among companies with established products for sale

Failing to recognise the time required for a successful development programme

Failing to focus the search correctly

Failing to investigate prior to production

Overlooking opportunities by using 'mechanical' screening procedures

Failure to obtain qualified outside assistance when needed

Too much analysis and too little action; or *vice versa*

5.5.2 Anticipated sales for 1982

| | Value, £'000 | Unit sales | | | Moving annual total of value, £'000 |
		Music systems	Cabinets complete	Other	
January	275	246	14	15	1,815
February	270	222	28	20	1,855
March	230	221	8	1	1,895
April	180	115	50	15	1,905
May	170	103	52	15	1,925
June	170	103	50	17	1,970
Total 6 mths	1,295	1,010	202	83	
July	135	135	—	—	2,005
August	90	85	5	—	2,005
September	160	130	30	—	2,050
October	170	103	62	5	2,070
November	180	150	24	6	2,100
December	170	152	9	9	2,200
Total 12 months	2,200	1,765	332	103	

The data shown as 'Moving annual total of sales' is used in compiling the graphical presentation shown in Section 10.6.3 and the 'Monthly value of sales' is used in presenting the seasonal pattern of sales graphs in Section 10.6.2.

Is ratio of contracts/orders received to quotations submitted:
  increasing?
  static?
  decreasing?

Do we quantify needs and degree of interest of enquirer?

Do we establish?
  Whether quotation is for future reference?
  Whether purchase depends upon other negotiations?
  A firm intent to purchase?
  When completion/delivery is required?
  Competitive involvement?
  Maximum price?
  Clear understanding of requirements?
  Probability of successful negotiations?
  A provisional estimate prior to full quote?

Define the size and type of quotation which should not require executive involvement

Institute a standard follow-up procedure – by correspondence/telephone

Submit reports of progress towards completion of negotiations

Quotations:

Does the layout and general appearance of our quotations compare favourably with that of our competitors?

For certain low-priced quotations, consider image, may appear too expensive to the customer?

Are any people singularly successful in converting quotations into firm orders – if so, analyse methods used

In the event of a contract or order being lost, obtain the true reason for failure

Indicate Conditions of Sale on every written quotation

Endeavour to make 'on site' quotations for low-cost work and seek additional work at same time

Completion of reports:

Do not waste management time by writing superfluous and unusable information, but do transmit essential information for prompt action

Reports from salesmen can show:
  Value of sales
  Number of sales
  Category of sale
  Sales target per period
  Attainment towards target
  Number of calls made
  Number of new prospects found
  Reason for no sale
  Length of each interview
  Quality of prospect
  Number and date of return calls
  New accounts opened
  Name and address of all calls
  Complaints
  Enquiries
  Request for quotations
  Progress on enquiries/quotations
  Competitive activity

Analysis of reports:

Use reports and records of salesmen to reveal average:
  Call rate
  Length of interview
  Percentage of travelling time
  Value of orders

Numbers of enquiries passed from head office

Conversion ratio of orders to enquiries

Are sales territory boundaries clearly defined?

Are maps of sales territories issued to salesmen?

Are sales territories in line with possible increase of salesmen?

Calculate the 'new business' potential in possible expanding areas

The Financial Director in conjunction with the other executive directors prepares the expected results for 1982 taking into account the answers to the questions in Section 5.6.1.

Is the corporate plan capable of measurement in financial terms?

Do the company objectives reconcile with the plan?

Are all areas of income and cost being made the responsibility of an individual?

Are any gaps apparent in the information to be consolidated?

Is the basis of cost allocation effective?

Are levels of authority regarding cost commitment adequate?

How often will internal procedures be examined conscientiously?

How flexible is the total control system to accommodate special circumstances?

Are existing bank and other cash resources adequate for the period under consideration?

Have any special conditions been imposed by bankers or other major suppliers?

Are relationships with major suppliers sound?

Have acceptable credit terms been negotiated with major customers and suppliers?

Has the company a contingency plan to cover a financial crisis?

Is a longer-term financial plan covering a period of up to three years advisable?

Will expansion necessitate the introduction of further funds?

Will this be available from existing sources or will new capital be introduced from other sources?

Can the management information system be designed to monitor and produce relevant control data?

Does the consolidated plan 'look right' within the limited planning horizon?

How will the plan be formally adopted as a budget?

On whom will the responsibility fall to communicate the budget to the lowest cost centre?

Will the communication system be examined periodically?

Leisure Sound Limited
Profit and loss account for the year ended 31 December

	1982 budgeted £'000	1981 actual £'000
Sales	2,200	1,800
Stock at January 1982	230	200
Purchases	1,035	711
	1,265	911
Deduct: stock at 31 December 1982	350	236
Cost of materials	915	675
Overheads and other expenditure	960	940
Depreciation	65	40
Total cost of sales	1,940	1,655
Profit before tax	260	145
Taxation	125	75
Profit after tax	135	70
Dividend	45	40
Retained and added to reserves	90	30

Leisure Sound Limited
Net Assets at 31 December

	1982 budget £'000	1981 actual £'000
Fixed assets		
Goodwill	120	120
Plant and machinery	250	270
Fixtures and fittings	45	40
Motor vehicles	80	80
	495	510
Net current assets		
Stock	350	236
Trade debtors	235	220
Current assets	585	456
Trade creditors	240	190
Bank overdraft	30	80
Taxation	125	110
Proposed dividend	45	40
Current liabilities	440	420
	145	36
Net assets	640	546
Capital employed		
Share capital	400	400
Reserves	70	36
Retained profit	90	30
	160	66
Shareholder's funds	560	466
Long-term loans	80	80
Capital employed	640	546

Leisure Sound Limited
Cash flow statement for year to 31 December 1982

	Budget, £'000
Revenue	
Profit before taxation	264
Taxation	(110)
Dividend	(40)
Increase in net current assets	
Stock	(114)
Debtors	(15)
Creditors	50
Net inflow	35
Capital	
Capital expenditure	(50)
Long-term loan	—
Depreciation	65
Net inflow	15
Bank balance	
(Net outflow)	—
Net inflow	50
Bank overdraft at 1 January 1982	(80)
Bank overdraft at 31 December 1982	(30)

Does the budget anticipate the attainment of the minimum criteria as laid down in Section 4.2?

	Actual for 1981	Required for 1982	Budget for 1982
Sales growth, %	16.1	22.0	22.2
Minimum profit after depreciation, £'000	145	260	260
Net profit margin on sales, %	8.1	11.5	11.8
Minimum return on year end net assets, %*	20.0	30.0	32.5

*Net assets for the purposes of this calculation exclude interest payable and bank borrowings, taxation and proposed dividends.

5.6.4 Budgeting principles checklist

The following checklist was used to consider the budgeting principles.

Budgeting:
- Is a management tool
- Is essential for short-term operational planning and control
- Aims to anticipate change

Budgetary control system conditions depend on the following:
- Management responsibility must be clear
- Managers must see their standards and budgets as attainable
- The budgetary control information must be understood by those for whom it is designed
- Training in budgetary control must be effective
- The organisation of information production must be appropriate
- Managers must understand the purposes of the budgetary system

Budgets translate plans into firm parameters in terms of resource generation and utilisation in all areas against which performance can be continually monitored. Budgets can be for any period and cover the main operating areas, e.g.:
- Profit and loss statements in detail
- Asset movement:
    fixed assets including buildings, machinery, etc.
    stocks and work-in-progress
    debtors
    total assets
- Sales, orders received and orders on hand
- Manpower
    direct and indirect by function
    direct and indirect by product
    direct and indirect by division
- Remuneration:
    direct and indirect by function
    budget for standard hours available
- Stock analysis
    by category (e.g. pre-process, work in progress and finished goods)
    labour input
    material input
    write-down and other provisions
- Expense classification, e.g.
    remuneration
    commissions
    purchased services
    insurance
    depreciation
    energy
- Gross margin analysis by products
- Expense analysis by function and category:
    manufacturing
    assembly
    marketing
- Capital expenditure by project
- Sales analysis by class of customer and product
- Analysis of floor space
- Analysis of reserves
- Balance sheet
- Cash flow
- Analysis of research and development
- Projects
- Manufacturing shop loading and manpower utilisation

Does the budgeting process have top management sponsorship and support?

Is the budgeting process seen as being a major tool of management rather than an accounting technique?

Can responsible individuals throughout the organisation work to budgets?

Is management by objectives (MBO) practised? If so, do managers meet their objectives and if not, why not?

Are the figures in budget compiled on the basis of the same definitions as the actual figures with which they will be compared?

Does the budgeting process encourage delegation?

Do budgets motivate people in the desired direction?

Do all employees – and especially supervisors and managers – fully understand the cost implications of their work and are they able to plan cost expectations accordingly?

Do the budget targets lead to objective attainment?

Is the budget used as a tool for co-operative planning and control rather than as an inflexible tool of dominance?

Is balance achieved between budgeting for short-run operations and planning long-term strategy?

Are plans explicit?

Are plans understood?

Are plans capable of being adapted to meet change?

Who will be affected by future plans and how will these people be affected?

Are plans (and objectives) compatible with internal and external constraints?

Are plans capable of being monitored, i.e. in quantified format?

Is the time period covered by the budget related to the necessity for, and the possibility of, effective management action?

Has consideration been given to adopting rolling budgeting as opposed to purely periodic budgeting?

Is the budget built on a thorough knowledge of cost behaviour patterns?

Are budgeted expenditures classified in sufficient detail and over sufficient headings to permit the estimating of costs by each major item and function under each area of responsibility?

Do budget control reports include reasons as well as results?

Is control effort focused on significant deviations from plan only?

Are responsible individuals able to help in developing cost targets for themselves and their subordinates?

Is the staff function in the budgeting process carefully distinguished from the manufacturing and assembly function?

Is budgeting part of the duties of the management accountant? If not, why not and if so, are his terms of reference widely known?

Are forecasting procedures being developed?

Is the whole planning/budgeting endeavour based on a careful and continuing evaluation of all major factors (both external and internal) that will affect the future?

Is imagination used in identifying other courses of action prior to their evaluation in relation to corporate objectives?

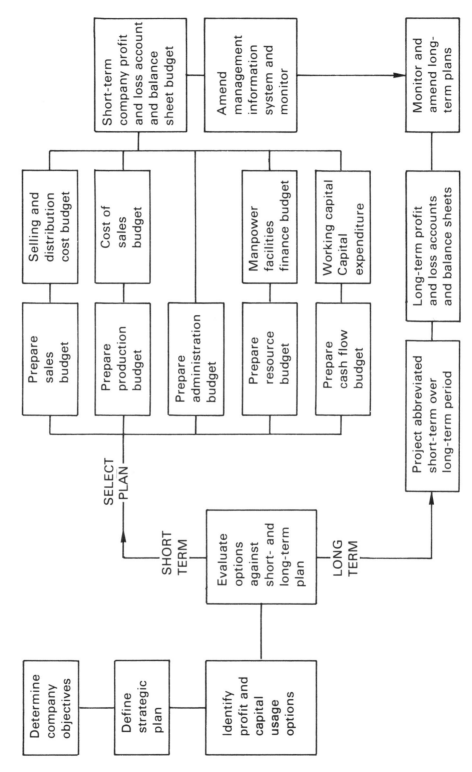

5.6.5 Budgetary control procedures

Determine company objectives → Define strategic plan → Identify profit and capital usage options → Evaluate options against short- and long-term plan

SHORT TERM → SELECT PLAN

LONG TERM → Project abbreviated short-term over long-term period

Prepare sales budget → Selling and distribution cost budget

Prepare production budget → Cost of sales budget

Prepare administration budget

Prepare resource budget → Manpower facilities finance budget

Prepare cash flow budget → Working capital Capital expenditure

Short-term company profit and loss account and balance sheet budget → Amend management information system and monitor → Monitor and amend long-term plans

Long-term profit and loss accounts and balance sheets

5.6.6 Budget approval and adoption

The budget, being in line with the company's requirements, is adopted.

6 Monitoring actual performance

Define information requirement before the year commences and use the defined requirement to design management information systems.

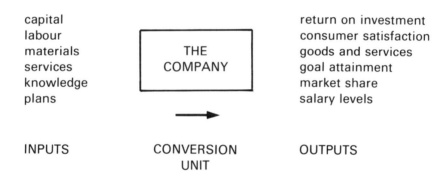

capital		return on investment
labour		consumer satisfaction
materials	THE	goods and services
services	COMPANY	goal attainment
knowledge		market share
plans		salary levels
INPUTS	CONVERSION UNIT	OUTPUTS

The purpose of a management accounting system is:

To show the cost structure of each product and process so that effective control may be exercised.

To facilitate product costing, for inventory valuation and income determination purposes.

To identify profit or loss by department, process or job – this can aid in determining the output or products that will lead to the most profitable level of operations.

To aid in the pricing decision by distinguishing between fixed and variable costs, thereby establishing lowest price levels.

To prevent wastage by the use of an efficient system of stores and wages control.

To provide cost estimate data on which to base tenders.

To secure more efficient operations, and more effective use of resources, by comparison of results with pre-determined standards (variance analysis) or data supplied by similar firms.

To permit the establishing of uniform cost accounting systems for inter-firm comparison purposes.

To identify and permit acceptable resource allocation.

To measure management accountability.

To enable *accountability* and *responsibility* to be measured.

6.2 TYPES OF REPORTS IN A MANAGEMENT INFORMATION SYSTEM

Profitability reports by:
  product
  division
  area
  customer group
  channel of distribution
  organisation
  profit responsibility centre

Cost reports of:
  labour analyses – direct and indirect
  productive labour variances
  non-productive labour variances
  direct expense analysis
  productivity analysis – direct labour
  overtime payment analysis
  analysis of spoilt work, rework and scrap
  material analysis
  manufacturing overhead analysis
  administrative cost analysis
  marketing cost analysis (order-getting costs)
  distribution cost analysis (order-filling costs)
  product costs
  cost of production
  cost of sales
  cost analyses for every responsibility centre
  and their constituent cost centres

Sundry reports on:
  orders received
  orders delivered
  overdue deliveries
  backlog of orders at month-end
  material yields
  cash receipts
  physical output
  research and development progress report
  special studies
  analysis and interpretation of problems
    or trends indicated by other regular
    reports
  studies directed towards finding cost-reduc-
    tion opportunities

Selection of reports depends upon:
  style of management
  management structure
  type of industry
  degree of flexibility available in manufac-
    turing process
  efficiency of information system
  financial vulnerability of company

The management information reporting system should be designed to follow the management structure and its lines of accounting.

Executive responsible	Frequency of reports			
	Weekly	Monthly	Quarterly	Annually
Departmental Managers:				
Manufacturing				
Assembly				
Distribution and trans- port				
Data — activity report	x	x		
Production Director:				
Data — activity report	x	x	x	
— Department costs	x	x	x	
Sales & Mktg Director:				
Data — Salesforce activity report		x		x
— Department costs		x		x
— Customer report			x	x
— Competitor report			x	x
Personnel Director				
Data — Employee efficiency and avail- ability report	x			
— Department costs		x		
Finance Director:				
Data — Department costs		x	x	x
— All dept. reports		x	x	x
— Actual/budget company accounts			x	x
Chief Executive:				
Data — Company profit and loss				
— Balance sheet			x	x
— Cash flow			x	x
— Directors' depart- mental summary		x	x	x
— Cash control state- ment		x	x	x

6.4 BASIC REASONS FOR REPORTING CONTROL DATA

The management information system must provide information that enables managers:

- To measure their effectiveness
- To discharge their stewardship
- To measure actual performance against a predetermined plan or budget
- To take corrective action whenever necessary

The information provided must be:

- Understandable
- Timely
- Accurate to acceptable tolerances for the purpose which it serves
- Constantly reviewed and appraised
- Supportive of the managers' tasks
- Produced economically
- Enable rapport to be established between all functions of the operation

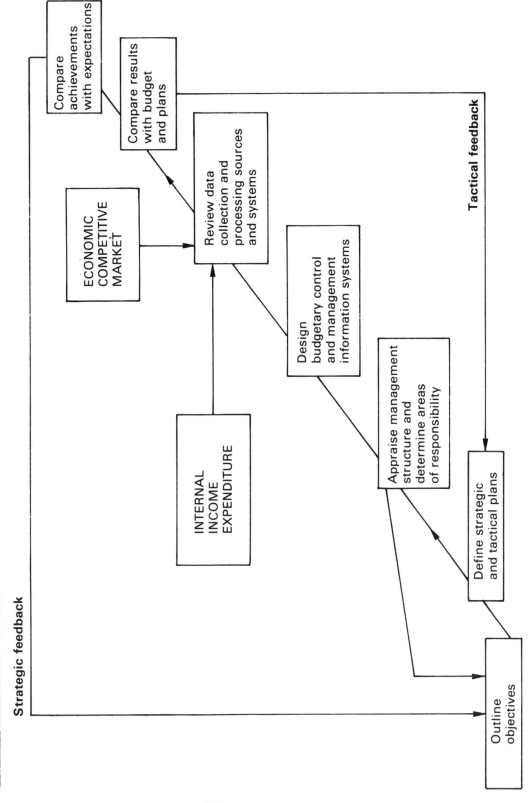

6.4.1 Management information systems cycle

Strategic feedback

Tactical feedback

Compare achievements with expectations

Compare results with budget and plans

ECONOMIC COMPETITIVE MARKET

Review data collection and processing sources and systems

INTERNAL INCOME EXPENDITURE

Design budgetary control and management information systems

Appraise management structure and determine areas of responsibility

Define strategic and tactical plans

Outline objectives

Establish a budget and monitor performance.

Monitary requirements: measure actual against budget for
   Numbers employed
   Available production capacity
   Efficiency of workforce
   Costs of manufacture
   Costs of assembly
   Level of raw material stock
   Level of manufactured stock
   Level of assembled stock
   Profitability of production/assembly departments
   Administration and other overhead costs
   Personal accountability for costs
   Storage and distribution costs
   Sales and effectiveness of sales force
   Total funds utilised in productive and other assets
   Effectiveness of control of investment in working capital
   Total profitability of company.

Identifying required remedial action, assign personal responsibility and measure effectiveness of ultimate action.

7 Management control information

The information that must be available to the department's manager must enable him to discharge his responsibilities as laid down by his superior and probably approved at a higher level of authority.

The requirements relating to the presentation of information are:
- simplicity
- readily understandable
- provide information essential for decision-taking
- have the manager's involvement in initial design
- control data extracted and reconciled from management information system
- sufficient information without recourse to other sources for supplementary data
- designed for handwritten or typewritten compilation
- established distribution list

Information requirement for control forms in Sections 7.1.1 and 7.1.2:
- number of employees
- level of employee efficiency
- available machine hours
- lost time for machine breakdown or maintenance
- units produced
- unit costs and variance from budget cost
- value of stock and number of weeks cover for projected sales
- number of weeks unit orders on hand

111

Leisure Sound Ltd

Weekly control sheet

Cabinet Shop	Period: 4 13 Weeks to 1 April 1982					Period total	Period budget	Variance	Cumulative variance to date
	Weeks								
	1	2	3	4	5				
Personnel: Number of employees	10	9	10						
Activity ratio, %	94	97	95						
Employee/unit ratio, (no.)	56	61	61						
Activity: Capacity m/c hours	85	85	85						
Available m/c hours	80	72	80						
Worked m/c hours	75	70	76						
Weekly production, units	560	565	565						
Value of production, £	2,240	2,220	2,260						
Unit cost, £ Material	4.06								
Employment	1.02	_etc._							
Energy	0.178								
Maintenance & depreciation	0.536								
	5.792								
Overheads	4.393								
Total cost	10.185	_etc._							
Selling/transfer price Profit/(loss) margin									
Budget total cost	9.75								
Variance/unit	(0.435)	_etc_							
Stock: Value of material Weeks production No. of finished units									
Orders: External Internal									
No. of weeks production									

Completed control sheet for 5 weeks of Period 3 is given in Section 7.1.2

Leisure Sound Ltd
Weekly control sheet

Cabinet Shop	Period: *3* *13* Weeks to *1 April 1982*								
	Weeks					Period total	Period budget	Variance	Cumulative variance to date
	1	*2*	*3*	*4*	*5*				
Personnel:									
Number of employees	*10*	*9*	*10*	*10*	*10*				
Activity ratio, %	*94*	*97*	*95*	*95*	*93*	*94.8 ave*	*95.0 ave*	*(0.2)*	*—*
Employee/unit ratio, (no.)	*56*	*61*	*61*	*60*	*55*	*293*	*300*	*(7)*	*(18)*
Activity:									
Capacity m/c hours	*85*	*85*	*85*	*85*	*85*	*425*	*425*		
Available m/c hours	*80*	*72*	*80*	*80*	*80*	*392*	*400*	*(8)*	*(26)*
Worked m/c hours	*75*	*70*	*76*	*76*	*74*	*371*	*380*	*(9)*	*(21)*
Weekly production, units	*560*	*549*	*610*	*600*	*550*	*2,869*	*3,000*	*(131)*	*(330)*
Value of production, £	*2,240*	*2,196*	*2,440*	*2,400*	*2,120*	*11,496*	*12,000*	*(504)*	*(1,200)*
							Average values		
Unit cost, £									
Material	*4.06*	*4.10*	*Completed as required*			*4.08*	*4.10*	*0.02*	*(0.08)*
Employment	*1.02*	*1.09*				*1.12*	*1.00*	*(0.12)*	*(0.41)*
Energy	*0.178*	*0.18*				*0.19*	*0.18*	*(0.01)*	*(0.02)*
Maintenance & depreciation	*0.536*	*0.56*				*0.55*	*0.502*	*(0.44)*	*(1.51)*
	5.792	*5.93*				*5.94*	*5.78*	*(0.16)*	*(1.86)*
Overheads	*4.393*	*4.31*				*4.39*	*4.22*	*(0.17)*	*(0.99)*
Total cost	*10.185*	*10.24*				*10.33*	*10.00*	*(0.33)*	*(2.85)*
Selling/transfer price	*6.00*	*6.00*				*6.00*	*6.00*	*—*	*—*
Profit/(loss) margin	*(4.185)*	*(4.24)*				*(4.33)*	*(4.00)*	*—*	*—*
Budget total cost	*9.725*	*9.725*				*9.725*	*9.725*		
Variance/unit	*(0.46)*					*(0.605)*	*(0.275)*		
Stock:									
Value of material						*£13,776*	*£14,000*	*£224*	
Weeks production						*6*	*7*	*1*	
No. of finished units						*400*	*375*	*(25)*	
Orders:									
External						*1,050*	*1,500*	*(450)*	
Internal						*6,000*	*7,000*	*(1,000)*	
No. of weeks production						*12.2*	*14.2*	*(2.0)*	

7.1.3 Manufacturing department checklist

Is the layout of the forms and disclosures generally compatible with the criteria in Section 6.5?

Is it necessary to budget this department on a weekly basis or will monthly or period budgeting suffice?

Is availability of workforce critical to the department's efficiency; should the personnel department be appraised of the workforce situation daily?

Has the departmental manager the responsibility to take corrective action over workforce when appropriate?

If budget information is not required on a weekly basis should production targets be set daily or weekly?

Is it necessary to establish weekly the efficiency of the department?

Will corrective action arise from this information?

Should separate records be maintained on each individual's level of efficiency, both numbers produced and numbers rejected?

Could renumeration systems be tied to individual efforts, or should the manufacturing activity be considered as a single unit?

Can the actual capacity hours, i.e. the maximum possible productive hours available taking into account production bottlenecks and individual machine speeds, be calculated on a consistent basis from week to week?

Are changes in equipment logged and capacity hours altered appropriately?

How often are detailed studies undertaken to check the levels of capacity hours?

What accounts for the difference between capacity hours and available hours?

What action should be taken to remedy any controllable lost hours, e.g. machine breakdown?

Does any discussion and training take place on a regular basis at supervising levels to consider problems of lost production?

How often are employees made aware of problem areas and achievements? Should this be on a regular basis? Should it be on a collective or individual basis?

Are costs in line with budgeted costs?

Where variances arise are the materials and the variances controllable in succeeding periods?

How often are cost data reconciled with the total company system?

Are adequate reasons given for variances likely to impact on profitability?

Is sufficient raw material stock in hand to fulfil outstanding orders?

How many weeks' production is in hand and what action is necessary if below the minimum required?

Generally:

Do adequate standards exist?

Are all processing operations necessary?

Could alternative processes be used to advantage?

Could existing processes be simplified?

Is the sequence of operations the best possible?

Is idle time between operations at a minimum?

Do any operations result in excessive rejects?

Are workloads planned sufficiently far in advance to permit workforce and machines to be balanced?

Are records of rejects maintained for combined purposes?

Is the inventory of maintenance spares adequate?

The information which must be available to the department's manager must enable him to discharge his responsibilities as laid down by his superior and probably approved at a higher level of authority.

The requirements relating to the presentation of information are:
- simplicity
- readily understandable
- provide information essential for decision-taking
- have the Manager's involvement in initial design
- control data extracted and reconciled from Management information system
- sufficient information without recourse to other sources for supplementary data
- designed for handwritten or typewritten compilation
- established distribution list

Information requirement for control forms in Sections 7.2.1 and 7.2.2:
- number of employees
- level of employee efficiency
- available assembly hours
- units assembled
- unit costs and variance from budget cost
- value and number of unit stock

Leisure Sound Ltd

| Weekly control sheet: | *Week 3* | | | | | | | | Department *Speaker Assembly* | | |

	Period 5 5 week(s) to 31 May 1982									Cumu-lative variance to date
	Weeks					Period				
	1	2	3	4	5	Total	Budget	Var-iance		
Personnel:										
Number of employees	8	8	7							
Activity ratio. %	97	97	96							
Employee/unit ratio	122.5	125.0	122.3							

	1	2	3	4	5	Total	Budget	Variance	Cumulative
Activity:									
Maximum assembly hours	320	320	280						
Available assembly hours	310	318	275						
Worked assembly hours	310	310	270			*The completed control sheet for 5 weeks of Period 5 is given in Section 7.2.2*			
Standard assembly units	1020	1020	892						
Actual assembly units	980	1000	856						
Assembly variance, hr	(10)	(10)	(10)						
Assembly variance, %	(3)	(3)	(3.5)						
Production efficiency variance:									
Units	(40)	(20)	(36)						
Percentage	96	98	95						

	£	£	£	£
Unit cost: Transfers in				
Employment				
Energy				
Maintenance and depreciation				
Overheads				
Total cost:				
Assembled unit cost				
Budgeted unit cost				

Stock: Cabinets			
Speakers: A			
B			
C			
Week production			
Completed units			

Leisure Sound Ltd

| Weekly control sheet: Week 5 | | | | | | Department Speaker Assembly | | | |

	Weeks					Period			Cumulative variance to date
	1	2	3	4	5	Total	Budget	Variance	
Personnel:									
Number of employees	8	8	7	7	8				
Activity ratio, %	97	97	96	89	94	94.6	97.1	(2.5)	(4.0)
Employee/unit ratio	122.5	125	122.3	113.4	121.3	120.9	130.9	(10)	(14)
Activity:									
Maximum assembly hours	320	320	280	280	320	1520	1520	—	—
Available assembly hours	310	318	275	280	300	1483	1500	(17)	(60)
Worked assembly hours	310	310	270	250	300	1440	1475	(35)	(135)
Standard assembly units	1020	1020	892	892	1020	4844	4844	—	—
Actual assembly units	980	1000	856	794	970	4600	4800	(200)	(810)
Assembly variance, hr	(10)	(10)	(10)	(30)	(20)	(80)	(45)	(35)	(135)
Assembly variance, %	(3)	(3)	(3.5)	(10.7)	(6.25)	(5.2)	(3.0)	(2.2)	(4.7)
Production efficiency variance:									
Units	(40)	(20)	(36)	(98)	(50)	(244)	(44)	(200)	(810)
Percentage	96	98	95	89	95	95	99	(4)	98

Unit cost:	£	£	£	£
Transfers in	8240	8380	140	660
Employment	1440	1520	80	380
Energy	185	170	(15)	(60)
Maintenance and depreciation	21	22	1	—
	9886	10092	206	980
Overheads	600	620	20	85
Total cost:	10 486	10 712	226	**1065**
Assembled unit cost	2.279	—	(0.047)	(0.051)
Budgeted unit cost	—	2.232		

Stock:				
Cabinets	8200	9000	800	
Speakers: A	8000	8000		
B	7600	10000	2400	
C	15000	10000	(5000)	
Week production	7.5	7.8	(0.3)	
Completed units	4200	4000	(200)	

117

Is the layout of the forms and disclosures generally compatible with the criteria in Section 6.5?

Is it necessary to budget this department on a weekly basis or will monthly or period budgeting suffice?

Is availability of workforce critical to the department's efficiency? Should the personnel department be appraised of the workforce situation daily?

Has the departmental manager the responsibility to take corrective action over workforce when appropriate?

If budget information is not required on a weekly basis should assembly targets be set daily or weekly?

Is it necessary to establish weekly the efficiency of the department?

Will corrective action arise from this information?

Should separate records be maintained on each individual's level of efficiency, both numbers assembled and numbers rejected?

Could renumeration systems be tied to individual efforts, or should the assembly activity be considered as a single unit?

Can the actual capacity hours, i.e. the maximum possible assembly hours available taking into account assembly bottlenecks and parts available, be calculated on a consistant basis from week to week?

Are changes in equipment logged and maximum hours altered appropriately?

How often are detailed studies undertaken to check the levels of possible hours?

What accounts for the difference between maximum assembly hours and available assembly hours?

What action should be taken to remedy any controllable lost hours, e.g. availability of components?

Does any discussion and training take place on a regular basis at supervising levels to consider problems of lost production?

How often are employees made aware of problem areas and achievements? Should this be on a regular basis? Should it be on a collective or individual basis?

Are costs in line with budgeted costs?

Where variances arise are these material and are the variances controllable in succeeding periods?

How often are cost data reconciled with the total company system?

Are adequate reasons given for variances likely to impact on profitability?

Is sufficient raw material stock in hand to fulfil outstanding orders?

How many weeks' production is in hand and what action is necessary if below the minimum required?

Generally:

Do adequate standards exist?

Are all processing operations necessary?

Could alternative processes be used to advantage?

Could existing processes be simplified?

Is the sequence of operations the best possible?

Is idle time between operations at a minimum?

Do any operations result in excessive rejects?

Are workloads planned sufficiently far in advance to permit workforce and machines to be balanced?

Are records of rejects maintained for combined purposes?

Is the inventory of maintenance spares adequate?

Low stock investment *versus* high stock investment.

For low stock investment:

Stock easy to control
Small delivery loads
Easy to handle
Cost of storage low
Low capital investment
Lower risk of damage and loss
Quicker turnover of stock
Advantages of new quality and design
Better control of product costs

For high stock investment:

Flexibility in fixing production schedules
Cost advantage in inflationary conditions
Greater supervisory requirements
Stable product selling price
Minimum dependence on raw material suppliers
Minimum dependence on financial and commercial stability of component suppliers
Maintenance of design criteria
Avoidance of retraining requirements at assembly lines

Are supplies purchased in economic quantities?

Are incoming goods examined for quantity, quality and conformance to order?

Has an analysis been carried out to verify lead times used in reordering?

Are order points developed for each item on the basis of lead times, rates of usage and safety stocks?

What are the costs of carrying each type of inventory?

What are the costs of reordering items for inventory?

Where sales are seasonal is it more advisable to produce in accordance with demand, or to produce at an even rate, and use stocks as a buffer?

How much of inventory investment is in work-in-progress?

Are supply costs of consumable production materials properly isolated from general maintenance costs?

Are there safeguards against overstocking?

Do excessive material shortages arise?

Are obsolete supplies disposed of?

How much capital is tied up in obsolete materials/components?

Could excess stocks be sold in bulk with special discounts, or is it cheaper to allow high stocks to run down through normal usage?

Is there adequate protection against pilferage and wastage?

Is the most suitable materials handling equipment used?

Are containers compatible with storage and materials handling?

Are containers marked/coloured for easier segregation/identification?

Could materials be purchased in sizes or quantities that would make for easier materials handling?

Can materials be moved best by gravity or on rollers?

Is a conveyor justified?

Are the materials handling and manufacturing functions effectively co-ordinated?

Can operations be combined at one work station to reduce materials handling?

Are containers uniform to permit stacking?

Can palletised loads be used?

Are fork-lift trucks and pallets used to advantage?

If of value, are returnable containers properly accounted for and controlled?

Could a deposit system be used on returnable containers/pallets?

Are scrap and waste materials dealt with effectively?

The major factors in inventory acquisition are:

Purchased parts:
  purchasing department costs
  freight inwards
  receiving department costs
  incoming inspection
  portion of warehouse labour involved in putting away
  personnel involved in accounts payable

Manufactured parts:
  set-up labour
  start-up material and/or scrap
  first piece and later inspection
  cost of preparing a manufacturing order

Inventory carrying cost elements are:
  insurance
  taxes
  space
  material handling
  return on investment
  physical inventorying
  loss, damage and deterioration
  obsolescence
  economic trends
  optional miscellaneous items:
    record keeping and accounting
    management charges

General questions that need to be asked:

Are quotations obtained from a number of sources?

Are alternative suppliers approached?

Are all purchase requisition/purchase orders properly authorised?

Does a policy exist for inviting bids/estimates/tenders?

Are safeguards in existence to prevent the purchasing of excessive quantities?

Is the purchasing department given a sound forecast of materials and other requirements in good time to enable them to be bought on favourable items?

Are some components currently being made that could be bought from outside at less cost?

Ordering costs against stock-holding costs?

Financial questions that need to be asked:

What are the vendors' financial and credit ratings?

What credit terms are offered?

How do these compare with other suppliers' credit terms?

How do they compare with the suppliers' cash flow needs?

What are the cost implications of overdue deliveries?

Are make or buy studies undertaken?

Are the prices competitive (given quality levels)?

What controls do suppliers have over their activities?

Is standard costing employed?

Is sufficient information available by specific cost element to know the reasonableness of the price quoted?

Might past termination or redetermination data be helpful in analysing this procurement?

Is the price reasonable in terms of competition?

What is the supplier's current financial position as shown in the most recent balance sheet?

What are the supplier's current projected levels of business?

Are there additional sources of capital if they are needed (for the supplier)?

What type of accounting system is employed: job cost? standard cost? other?

Price breakdowns by cost element on fixed price contracts should be furnished.

Is there any objection to contracting on other than a fixed price basis?

Is special tooling being purchased separately?

Are there any mating interchangeability problems?

Should tooling be coded?

Are supplier's employees unionised? If so, when do union contracts expire?

Will designated individuals in engineering, production and finance be specified from whom the buyer can obtain pertinent information and data as he requires it?

Are all necessary activities included?

Are there any special handling, packaging or shipping requirements that may delay delivery?

Are spares involved, and are they allowed for in the vendor's plans and schedules?

Are all inspection, test, and engineering requirements fully understood?

Is the item adequately described on the specification, purchase order, etc?

Are there any special test or quality control requirements the vendor must meet?

Does he fully understand them, and does he have the time, facilities and know-how to comply?

Are sources accustomed to manufacturing this item?

Do they demonstrate ability to meet this schedule?

Do their past rejection experiences demonstrate ability to meet test and quality requirements?

Is a performance bond advisable?

Should the right be obtained to use or acquire tooling, designs, materials to manufacture the item in case of default?

7.4 SALES

The information which must be available to the department's manager must enable him to discharge his responsibilities as laid down by his superior and probably approved at a higher level of authority.

The requirements relating to the presentation of information are:
- simplicity
- readily understandable
- provide information essential for decision-taking
- have the manager's involvement in initial design
- control data extracted and reconciled from management information systems
- sufficient information without recourse to other sources for supplementary data
- designed for handwritten or typewritten compilation
- established distribution list

7.4.1 Sales weekly control form

Leisure Sound Ltd: Sales information report

Period Weeks to								Cumulative to								Year to		
Music system		Other		Total			Music system		Other		Total				Fore-cast		Vrnce
Units	£	Vrnce	£	Vrnce	£	Vrnce	Units	£	Vrnce	£	Vrnce	£	Vrnce		£	£	£

Sales
Area 1
Area 2
Area 3
Etc.

Profit contribution

Costs:
Marketing
Selling
Discounts
Packing
Distribution

Total cost

Net contribution

Unit margin
Number of salesmen
Cost per salesman
Customer/salesmen calls
Debtors outstanding
Number of days' credit

123

Is it essential to record and review sales on a product basis: actual sales compared with budgeted sales; unit and value by period, cumulative trend forecast?

Is it necessary to show profit margins by product category?

What is volume of repeat orders?

Is data relating to customers and territory available?

Is the extent to which variances have arisen from changes in volume known?

What would profitability be if sales were made out to distributors or factories?

Are controls on sales calls on customers justified?

By how much would profit contributions increase at varying levels of advertising and promotional expenditure?

Does the information disclosed permit comparison of marketing effort from one area to another?

Is the cost information relevant for changes in marketing strategy?

What is the volume of orders in hand for future delivery in relation to available production capacity?

Are salesmen conscious of profitable customers and concentration of effort?

Are salesmen's movements planned?

Do cash discounts result in over-rapid debt collection?

Are delivery schedules met? If not, are the reasons known and delays rectified?

Are stock levels adequate to provide the planned level of customer service?

Do sales forecasts take into account demand and productive capacity?

Are customer complaints analysed?

Are data retained to provide replacement-under-guarantee information?

What is the replenishment lead time?

What is the history of out-of-stock situations?

What stocks are normally held at the factory?

What stocks are normally in the distributor's pipeline?

7.5 PACKAGING, DISTRIBUTION AND TRANSPORT

7.5.1 Packaging checklist

Could lighter or lower-cost packaging be used?

Is shrink-wrapping possible with current advances in technology?

Is packaging design co-ordinated with materials handling?

Do all items need packaging?

Consider the following:

The duration and type of journey involved, and the strains involved.

The fragility or perishability of the goods transported.

The handling and stacking methods which will be employed at each change in mode.

The sensitivity of the goods to environment.

The unit value of the goods and how much packaging can be afforded.

The extent to which the goods have to be packaged for other reasons:

   the need for identification

   the desirability of not having to break down

   the package for final consignment

the desirability of separate items arriving together at the destination.

border documentation and customs requirements.

the need to stop pilfering.

limitations imposed by doors, hatches, cranes, statutory requirements, e.g. rail packaging regulations, IATA rules.

insurance requirements.

Leisure Sound Ltd: Packaging weekly control information

	Period		Weeks to			
	Weeks to		Cumulative weeks to		Year to	
	Actual	Budget variance	Actual	Budget variance	Actual	Budget variance
Received for packing, units Packed, units Packed/received, %						
Number of employees Capacity hours Worked hours Employee efficiency, %						

Costs:
  Packing material used
  Employment
  Other direct costs						

Overheads:
  Direct
  Apportioned						

Total packing cost						
Unit/packed cost						
Stock of packing material Weeks material in hand Unit packaging in hand						

7.5.3 Distribution and transport checklist

General considerations:

Number and type of call.

Capacity of vehicle and vehicle type.

Urbanisation and vehicle speeds obtainable.

Balance between driving time and delivery time.

Size of orders.

Distance between calls.

Maximum working day.

Shop or customer opening hours.

Road network.

Load layout and use of compartments for different products.

Maintenance of an adequate service level.

Logistic factors:

Volume of goods, inwards and outwards.

Regular deliveries or movements and frequencies.

Variable deliveries – variants and seasonal effects.

Trends – increasing or diminishing.

Customers' expectation of service.

Type of movement – factory to warehouse, first or second degree outlet or export.

Stock location:

Fixed location – bin storage, but this can waste space.

Random location – least unoccupied space, but increases search time.

Zoned location – fixed or random located within zones.

Warehouse action checklist:

Evaluate operating requirements of warehouse.

Study systems and improve where possible.

Construct job descriptions.

Perform work study exercise.

Implement recommendations and improve operating methods.

Develop incentive schemes where necessary.

Transport checklist:

Compare costs of company-owned transport function with outside contractors.

Are the best means of transport (cost and service viewpoints) used for different products?

Are increases in transport costs considered to be unavoidable and thus passed on to customers without studying the efficiency of transport activities?

Are *all* transport costs accounted for under the heading of transport?

Can those vehicles having disproportionately high operating costs (in relation to other vehicles of the same make, age, and capacity) be identified?

How are standards set in the transport sphere? (If there are no standards, should they be introduced?)

Is control over fuel exercised by having a bulk storage facility, or does the company rely on outside agencies?

Could the costs be reduced by hiring a fleet (contract or lease) rather than owning vehicles?

Is maintenance planned or available on a crisis basis?

Does the cost control system reveal the extent to which transport facilities are under-utilised?

Does an established procedure exist for scheduling and routine vehicles?

Does routing take into account different road types, urban areas?

Is the most expensive resource, e.g. driver or vehicle, the focus of attention?

Is the capacity constraint of the fleet, volume or weight? (Are the right sizes of vehicles in use?)

Can mechanical loading/unloading methods be employed with the type of vehicles in use?

How is performance measured? Which aspects of performance are measured: driver performance, driver utilisation, vehicle utilisation, delay time?

What follow-up results from the extraction of variances?

Who takes responsibility for the cost of special deliveries?

To what extent can use be made of existing forms/reports (log sheets, mileage records, etc.) in building up costs?

What exceptions should be made to the usual arrangements?

What vehicle types should work what routes?

What characteristics should the journey patterns and consequent vehicle schedules have?

What should be the maximum allowable time away from base?

What maintenance and replacement policy should be adopted in respect of the vehicles?

During what hours should the depots, warehouses and factory despatch points operate?

On what routes, with which vehicles and under what circumstances should multiple shift working of the transport fleet take place?

How much staff and labour is required to operate the transport fleet, the warehouses, the depots, the factory despatch points?

Is the adopted management structure the most suitable?

Where should 'picking and packing' of customer orders take place?

What arrangements should be made for setting stock action levels and monitoring and allocating stocks?

What arrangements should be made for physical process of raising customers' orders, acknowledgements, despatch notes, etc.?

What other control documentation and procedures are required?

What is the broad specification of the management information system required?

Leisure Sound Ltd: Distribution and transport weekly control information

	Period	Weeks to				
	Weeks to		Cumulative weeks to		Year to	
	Actual	Budget variance	Actual	Budget variance	Actual	Budget variance
Vehicles owned: Commercial Private Vehicles in use: Commercial Private						
Commercial vehicles: Distance covered, miles Driver's hours at ordinary rate Mile/hour cost, £ Utilisation/ efficiency, %						
Actual hours at operative rate						
Costs: Fuel and oil Licence and insurance Employment (drivers) Vehicle repairs Employment (repair shop)						
Overheads: Direct: Transport Repair shop Apptnd: Transport Repair shop						
Total cost						

Cost per mile

Stock of parts, £
Average repair time
  per vehicle, hr

7.6 OVERHEAD DEPARTMENTS

7.6.1 Service department costs and allocation checklist

Overhead departments:

- Require to be managed.
- Require to be cost controlled.
- Require to provide an acceptable level of service at the lowest cost.
- Costs required to be apportioned to production/assembly departments.
- Costs must be included in all product costs.

The costs of service and other administration departments when allocated to production departments under either absorption or direct costing methods (Section 8.2.2) or a mixture of each must be allocated on a common sense basis (Section 8.2.5).

Depending on the style of management and where a system of responsibility accounting exists, control information must be designed to show:

- Total costs for which an individual manager is accountable.
- Total costs divided between directly controllable costs, e.g. employment, and those apportioned costs not directly controllable, e.g. rent.
- Total costs by function performed.
- Total costs recharged to other service or production departments.
- Adequate comparison against budget and explanation of variances from budget.
- Control information produced at regular intervals to enable corrective action to be taken.

8 Management information – monthly and quarterly

Avoid duplication.

Is information required in detail already disclosed?

Does it highlight the position at any point where control can be exercised?

Does it inform the reader of the salient points?

Does it condense the position to a manageable size?

If not, the information requirement will have to be related to the responsibilities of those for whom it is produced and the necessity for decision-taking.

A manager should be able to see from control data
- The total of the costs under the manager's control.
- The allocation of these costs between those which are controllable and those which are not.
- Variances from budget.
- The result of corrective action measured in money terms.
- The measurement of past performance as well as key information relating to the immediate future.
- Information in sufficient detail to enable future plans to be formulated within acceptable tolerance.

Should fixed costs and the costs of service departments be charged to production/ assembly departments?

What bases should be used for the charge?

If not charged, how should these costs be included within the selling price structure?

Absorption costing results in the inclusion of all or a proportion of all fixed costs in stock and work-in-progress values at either actual or a predetermined standard rate.

Direct costing has the effect of excluding all or a proportion of all fixed costs from the value of stock and work-in-progress, thereby including these costs from individual product costs.

A mix of the above methods may be appropriate in individual cases.

Considerations to be taken into account to identify the appropriate costing methods are as follows:

Absorption costing

Costs should be allocated to production/assembly departments on the basis of 'service rendered'.

Allocated costs should be added progressively to production/assembly costs where sequences of operations are involved.

Allocated costs must be included within the expense rate for each operation.

Since some expenses do not vary with volume change, actual expense rates will increase with volume decrease and decrease with volume increase.

Expense rates are usually based on the expense budget developed for control of expenditure which may differ from actual expenditure.

Appointment of costs have to be related to estimated 'normal' volumes of production/assembly.

Differences can arise when the total actual expenditure is related to the total absorbed expenditure. The difference is due to two factors: *control*, spending more than allowed for in the budget, and *volume*, a level of production/assembly different from that budgeted.

Realistic expense rates must be developed that will provide a sound pricing policy for existing and new products.

Allocated costs tend to distort the profitability of individual products.

When assessing overall company profitability

the contribution from all products and departments must be taken into account simultaneously.

Absorption costing obscures the total value of certain expenditure in internal reports.

Direct costing

Fixed expenditure is charged directly against the profit for a period.

Profits for a period are not affected by changes in the absorption of fixed expenditure resulting from an increase or reduction in stock and work-in-progress levels.

Avoids the necessity to apportion costs on an arbitrary basis.

Fluctuation in profit is easier to explain.

The contribution from each product can be identified.

The effects on profits of changes in selling price can be computed simply by calculating the effect on the marginal balance in the net sales income and direct costs.

Fixed expenditure is recorded and highlighted by appearing in internal reports.

Management accountability for the control of fixed expenditure is made simpler.

The procedure for monitoring costs under the direct costing method is less costly to operate.

8.2.3 Levels of activity relating to costs

What level of activity should be used in determining factory expense ratio?

What is normal volume on which to base an acceptable recovery rate?

If fixed expenses are allocated to products or assembly costs can the quantum of costs be distorted?

Is the process of allocating direct fixed costs more suitable for the products manufactured as opposed to those bought in?

Can profits be distorted from period to period by the application of either absorption or direct costing?

Is it essential to identify fixed costs for personal accountability?

Does the system of management accountability lend itself easier to either method of costing expenses?

Does the inclusion of fixed costs under the application of absorption costing distort the comparison of the relative profitability of products or departments?

Which method of costing application is commonly used within the industry?

Could it be more effective to apply a mixture of both absorption and direct costing?

Does the system of financial control in use affect the choice of which system should be used?

Does the range of products manufactured or assembled affect the choice of costing system to be applied?

Is the proportion of fixed costs high in relation to total costs?

With a shortfall in anticipated volumes what would be the effect on profitability under each costing method?

8.2.4 Different applications of costing systems

Company X manufacturing two articles within an accounting period

	Direct costing		Absorption costing	
	A, £	B, £	A, £	B, £
Sales:				
2 at £500 each (a)	1,000		1,000	
1 at £500 (b)		500		500
Cost of sales:				
Direct material, 2 at £100	200	200	200	200
Direct labout, 2 at £50	100	100	100	100
Production overheads, 2 at £75	150	150	150	150
Allocated overheads (£45 + 30 + 25)	—	—	100	100
	450	450	550	550
Deduct Value of stock (carried forward)	—	225	—	275
Net cost of sales	450	225	550	275
Gross surplus	550	275	450	225
Overheads:				
Selling (less 30% = £45)	150	150	105	105
Administration (less 30% = £30)	100	100	70	70
General (less 50% = £25)	50	50	25	25
	300	300	200	200
Net surplus/loss (c)	250	(25)	250	25

Notes: Company manufacturing two articles within an accounting period
(a) assumes both articles sold within same accounting period
(b) assumes one article sold, one carried forward as stock to next accounting period
(c) profitability depends upon costing method used.

	Direct costing	Absorption costing
Material	100	100
Direct labour	50	50
Production overheads	75	75
Allocated overheads	—	50
Stock value carried forward	£225	£275

The effect of application of absorption costing is to carry forward in the stock valuation a proportion of indirect overheads as above.

Three broad categories:

Blanket method: where all expenses to be allocated are lumped together and charged to cost centres on some predetermined ratio of unit activity to total company or group activity. The bases used more commonly are total expenses, payroll, cost of sales, sales, cost of investment, or return on investment.

Individual method: where each category of expense to be allocated is charged out on an individual basis. The bases used include data processing to number of computer hours, legal expenses to direct staff hours and personnel department expenses to the recipient unit employee numbers.

Combination method: where certain identifiable expenses are charged out to cost centres on an individual basis; the remaining expenses are distributed on the blanket basis.

Advantages and disadvantages:

Blanket method:
    Relatively simple to administer
    Avoids distortions in charge out
    Easily understood
    Encourages economies in charge-out base,
       e.g. capital employed
    Charge out bears little relationship to service
       performed
    Charge out is arbitrary

Individual method:
    Corresponds more closely to actual services
       provided
    Less emotive to managers
    Overspending can be related to individual's
       responsibility
    Considerable administrative effort involved

    Charge outs give an impression of accuracy

Combination method:
    Permits allocation of costs on a more identifiable basis
    More closely represents the actual situation
    Imparts feeling of fairness
    Necessitates greater administrative and accounting effort

Guidelines relating to any cost allocation formula:

The allocation basis must be seen to be effective and equitable.

Managers must be aware of the formula used.

Managers must be encouraged to question allocated costs.

Managers must be encouraged to reduce allocated cost by effectively altering the base under their control, e.g. numbers employed.

The allocation must be adhered to in such a manner as will influence decision-taking.

8.2.6 Cost recording requirement

Is the company's costing system tailored to the company's needs?

Have cost centres been clearly defined?

Are the benefits of the system commensurate with its costs?

Are all costs classified into their direct and indirect, fixed and variable, controllable and uncontrollable, and separate and joint categories?

Is the behaviour of different costs understood in relation to changes in the level of activity?

Are cost reports made available promptly? How often? How quickly?

Could statements be presented earlier if more estimates were used? (Are estimating procedures reliable?)

Are figures rounded so that results are more easily understood?

Can any figure of small value be grouped?

Are the descriptions of reported items clear?

Are unusual items adequately explained?

Will further (or less) mechanisation affect the overhead of cost accounting?

Can the effectiveness of cost accounting procedures be improved?

Has sufficient thought been given to the type of costing system to use? (For example, standard costing, absorption costing, or marginal costing.)

Has the purpose for which costing is being performed been fully considered? (For example, pricing, product costing, cost control.)

Is the costing system adequate in determining the relative efficiencies and profitable divisions, processes, product lines, jobs?

Is the costing system adequate for the needs of EDP and operational research analysis?

Are ratios, graphs etc, used to supplement the figures produced by the costing system?

Is a satisfactory procedure being operated to price material issues from stores?

Are all withdrawals of stock and ordering of goods form outside suppliers duly authorised by requisitions?

Are job allocation numbers recorded against labour time, material usage, etc., in all cases?

Do employees understand the importance of recording the allocation of time to jobs? How are they encouraged to do this accurately?

What is the basis for apportionment of each service departments' costs? Is the most suitable basis selected in every case?

How are overheads absorbed into productive output? Is the most suitable basis used?

What action is taken on the basis of over or under-recovery of overheads?

Are normalised over-recovery rates used? If not, why not? For example, is the level of activity stable from month to month?

Have separate overhead rates been developed for fixed overhead costs and variable overhead costs?

Why are overheads absorbed (if they are absorbed)?

Is the contribution margin concept understood within the company?

Is cost-volume-profit analysis undertaken?

Is marginal costing undertaken?

Has the company's margin of safety ever been worked out?

Are the comparative advantages and disadvantages of marginal costing *versus* absorption costing fully appreciated?

Is the costing system closely geared to the type of production processes operated?

What role does cost accounting play in relation to special decision-making?

9 Summarised management control information

The company's trading budget for 1982 which showed a profit before tax at £260,000 (Section 5.6.2) must be detailed for management control purposes. The budget (p 138) summarising the position, would be available to the company's executives (Section 5.1.1).

Checklist

Does the profit equal that shown in the agreed budget?

Does the information disclosed comply with the management accountability structure?

Is credit given to manufacturing and assembly departments for work produced, whether sold or transfered to another department?

Are the expenses broken down into those directly controllable and those allocated?

Can the effect of applying an agreed allocation procedure be readily seen in financial terms?

Can apparently unfair allocations of expenses be monitored for action?

Does the information when produced greatly add to management decision-taking where actual is compared with budget?

Does the information disclosed invite questions relating to deviations from budget?

What additional information is necessary: percentages, ratios, etc?

Can the information be readily reconciled with monthly and other management information?

The information disclosed relates only to profits; is similar information relating to net assets required also?

Is it necessary to produce all relevant information? Will salient information suffice as in Section 9.2?

Leisure Sound Ltd

Budget income and expenditure for year to 31 December 1982

Production departments	Departmental income			Material	Controllable direct expenditure	Gross contribution	Non-controllable expenditure		Contribution
	Sales	Transfers	Total revenue (notional)				Direct	Allocated	
Cabinet shop	30,000	160,000	190,000	120,000	53,500	16,500	60,000	58,000	(101,500)
Speaker assembly	–	250,000	250,000	100,000	24,500	125,500	49,000	23,000	53,500
Cabinet assembly	70,000	650,000	720,000	360,000	24,000	336,000	49,000	50,000	237,000
Unit assembly	335,000	745,000	1,080,000	720,000	19,500	340,500	81,000	59,000	200,500
System assembly	1,765,000	(15,000)	1,750,000	1,405,000	12,000	333,000	49,000	114,500	169,500
	2,200,000	1,790,000	3,990,000	2,705,000	133,500	1,161,000	298,000	304,500	559,000
Unrealised profit in stock									–
									559,000
Overheads:									
Executive					18,000		18,000	–	
Administration					39,500		57,000	(49,000)	
Personnel					11,000		16,500	(16,000)	
Secretarial					2,500		28,000	(5,000)	
Finance and accounting					32,000		16,500	(15,000)	
Corporate development					6,500		8,000	–	
Production and maintenance					30,500		9,000	(29,500)	
Packing and selling					60,000		49,000	(75,000)	
Delivery and storage					41,500		162,000	(105,000)	
					241,500		362,000	(304,500)	299,000
Total overheads					375,000		650,000		
Net contribution									£260,000

Allocation to production department	Cabinet manufacture	Speaker assembly	Cabinet assembly	Unit assembly	Systems assembly	Total
Administration	7,000	6,000	12,000	6,000	18,000	49,000
Personnel	3,000	3,000	4,000	3,000	3,000	16,000
Secretarial	1,000	1,000	1,000	1,000	1,000	5,000
Finance and accounting	4,000	4,000	1,000	3,000	3,000	15,000
Production and maintenance	10,000	9,000	7,000	5,000	8,500	39,500
Packing and selling	11,000	–	15,000	19,000	30,000	75,000
Delivery and storage	22,000	–	10,000	22,000	51,000	105,000
	£58,000	23,000	50,000	59,000	114,500	304,500

Leisure Sound Ltd
Management account for year to 31 December 1982

£'000	External sales Actual	Var.	Total production Actual	Var.	Controllable expenditure Actual	Var.	Gross margin Actual	Var.	Non-controllable expenditure Actual	Var.	Overhead expenditure Actual	Var.	Net profit Actual	Var.	Remarks
Production centres:															*Comments on main features*
Cabinet shop	24	(6)	168	(22)	161	13	7	(9)	123	(5)			(116)	(14)	
Speaker assembly	–	–	240	(10)	119	6	121	(4)	71	1			50	(3)	
Cabinet assembly	64	(6)	704	(16)	373	11	331	(5)	99	–			232	(5)	
Unit assembly	300	(35)	1,020	(60)	698	41	312	(19)	144	(4)			178	(23)	
System assembly	1,700	(65)	1,700	(50)	1,250	167	450	117	168	(4)			283	113	
	2,088	(112)	3,832	(158)	2,601	238	1,231	80	605	(12)			627	68	
Unrealised inter-department profit in transfers													(26)	(26)	
													601	42	
Cost centres:															
Executive					18	1			16	–	34	–			
Administration					36	3			64	(7)	100	(4)			
Personnel					11	–			17	11	28	11			
Secretarial					2	1			17	–	19	1			
Finance and accounting					32	1			33	(17)	65	(17)			
Corporate development					6	–			8	–	14	1			
Production and maintenance					29	3			10	(1)	38	2			
Selling and despatch					58	2			50	(1)	108	1			
Storage and delivery					36	5			172	(10)	208	(5)			
					227	15			397	(25)	614	(10)			
Deduct: recovery from production centres											305	–	309	(10)	
											309	(10)			
Net profit before tax													292	32	

Var. = Actual variance from budget

Since each executive responsible for managing production or service departments will be in possession of control information suitably detailed, the company information required at executive level should be abbreviated.

What is the minimum information required?

Can the accounts be easily reconciled with other management data?

Is it necessary to retain identity of management accountability through established cost centres?

Can minimum disclosure prove misleading?

Is the approach too simplistic?

Are the shortcomings inherent in simplification understood?

Will a written report remove management concern?

How often will the layout of the form be critically appraised for change?

The control formats shown in Sections 9.3.1 and 9.3.2 are suitable for both manufacturing and assembly departments and combine essential control data against the checklists in Sections 7.1.3 and 7.1.4. The formats can be further refined against the checklist above as shown in Section 9.3.3.

Leisure Sound Ltd

Department account: *Cabinet Shop*

	Period ended: 31/12/82			Previous year	Cumulative to: 12 periods to 31/12/82			Previous year
	Actual	Budget	Variance	Variance	Actual	Budget	Variance	Variance
Units manufactured	2,458	2,625	(167)		31,000	32,000	(1,000)	
Units assembled	—	—		—	—	—	—	—
Production/capacity, %	87	93			98	96	2	
Orders on hand, units								
External	400	300	100					
Internal	2,600	2,700	(100)					
Total	3,000	3,000	—					
Units sold/transferred								
External sale					4,000	5,000	(1,000)	
Internal sale					24,000	26,666	(2,666)	
Total					28,000	31,666	(3,666)	
	£	£	£	£	£	£	£	£
Sales: external	1,835	2,600	(765)		24,000	30,000	(6,000)	
Sales: internal	10,800	14,200	(3,400)		144,000	160,000	(16,000)	
Total credits	12,635	16,800	(4,165)		168,000	190,000	(22,000)	
Deduct: Cost of sales								
Raw materials	10,020	10,000	(20)		112,000	120,000	8,000	
Bought-in parts	—	—	—		—	—	—	
Employment	2,416	2,458	42		28,500	29,500	1,000	
Energy	450	500	50		5,000	6,000	1,000	
Maintenance/depr'n	1,250	1,416	166		15,000	17,000	2,000	
Total	14,136	14,374	238		160,500	172,500	12,000	
Gross contribution	(1,501)	2,426	(3,927)		7,500	17,500	(10,000)	
Deduct:								
Rent	3,333	3,333	—		40,000	40,000	—	
Rates	2,250	1,500	(750)		25,000	18,000	(7,000)	
Personnel	375	250	(125)		4,000	3,000	(1,000)	
Finance/accounting	208	333	125		3,000	4,000	1,000	
Sec./insurance	83	166	83		1,000	2,000	1,000	
Admin.	460	583	123		6,000	7,000	1,000	
Bank interest	171	160	(11)		2,000	2,000	—	
Production control	833	850	17		10,000	10,000	—	
Packing & selling	1,080	920	(160)		12,000	11,000	(1,000)	
Storage & delivery	1,583	1,875	292		20,000	22,000	2,000	
Total	10,376	9,970	(406)		123,000	119,000	(4,000)	
Net contribution	(11,877)	(7,544)	(4,333)		(115,500)	(101,500)	(14,000)	

Leisure Sound Ltd

Department account: *Unit Assembly*

	Period ended: 31/12/82			Previous year	Cumulative to: 52 weeks ended 31/12/82			Previous year
	Actual	Budget	Variance	Variance	Actual	Budget	Variance	Variance
Units manufactured	—	—	—	—	—	—	—	—
Units assembled	1,600	1,700			20,000	20,000		
Production/capacity, %	92	95			96	98		
Orders on hand, units								
External	250	300	(50)					
Internal	980	1,200	(220)					
Total	1,230	1,500	(270)					
Units sold/transferred								
External sale					5,000	5,600	(600)	
Internal sale					12,000	12,400	(400)	
Total					17,000	18,000	(1,000)	
	£	£	£	£	£	£	£	£
Sales: external	26,660	28,000	(1,340)		300,000	335,000	(35,000)	
Sales: internal	58,330	63,750	(5,420)		720,000	745,000	(25,000)	
Total credits	84,990	91,750	(6,760)		1,020,000	1,080,000	(60,000)	
Deduct: Cost of sales								
Raw materials	—	—	—	—	—	—	—	
Bought-in parts	54,160	60,000	5,940		680,500	720,000	39,500	
Employment	1,125	1,210	85		13,000	14,000	1,000	
Energy	185	240	55		2,000	3,000	1,000	
Maintenance/depr'n	208	208	—		2,500	2,500	—	
Total	55,678	61,658	5,980		698,000	739,500	41,500	
Gross contribution	29,312	30,092	(780)		322,000	340,500	(18,500)	
Deduct:								
Rent	4,166	4,166	—		50,000	50,000	—	
Rates	2,500	2,500	—		30,000	30,000	—	
Personnel	710	250	(460)		8,000	3,000	(5,000)	
Finance/accounting	220	260	40		3,000	3,000	—	
Sec./insurance	83	83	—		1,000	1,000	—	
Admin.	417	500	83		5,000	6,000	1,000	
Bank interest	166	83	(83)		2,000	1,000	(1,000)	
Production control	416	416	—		5,000	5,000	—	
Packing & selling	1,701	1,585	(116)		20,000	19,000	(1,000)	
Storage & delivery	1,666	1,833	167		20,000	22,000	2,000	
Total	12,045	11,676	(369)		144,000	140,000	(4,000)	
Net contribution	17,267	18,416	(1,149)		178,000	200,500	(22,500)	

9.3.3 Sales and cost report

Leisure Sound Ltd: Sales and cost report, £'000

Department: Cabinet shop Manager: D. Jones Month: To 31 December 1982							
	Month ended 31 December 1982				Cumulative year to date		
	Actual	Budget	Variance		Actual	Budget	Variance
Sales: External Internal	1.8 10.8	2.6 14.2	(0.8) (3.4)		24.0 144.0	30.0 160.0	(6.0) (16.0)
TOTAL	12.6	16.8	(4.2)		168.0	190.0	(22.0)
Cost of sales: Material Controllable expenses	10.0 4.1	10.0 4.4	— 0.3		112.0 48.5	120.0 53.5	8.0 5.0
TOTAL	14.1	14.4	0.3		160.5	173.5	13.0
Other expenses: Non-controllable Allocated	6.2 4.2	5.7 4.3	(0.5) 0.1		67.0 56.0	60.0 58.0	(7.0) 2.0
TOTAL	10.4	10.0	(0.4)		123.0	118.0	(5.0)
TOTAL COST	24.5	24.4	(0.1)		283.5	291.5	8.0
NET CONTRIBUTION	(11.9)	(7.6)	(4.3)		(115.5)	(101.5)	(14.0)

143

9.4 MANAGEMENT INFORMATION BELOW EXECUTIVE LEVEL

The management control information suitable for executive weekly control is unsuitable for longer-time runs, e.g. quarterly and yearly. The information in the manufacturing and assembly departments is more suited for charge-hand or foreman level but not Production Director as a member of the management executive.

10 Results for 1982

Actual expenditure will be prepared and analysed as in Section 5.4.3. (Section 10.1).

The results will be prepared as in Section 5.6.2 and analysed (Section 10.2).

A summary of the financial achievement will be prepared to show main features of the year compared with previous years and budget (Section 10.3).

Leisure Sound Ltd
Actual expenditure by cost centre: year to 31 December 1982

Figures in £	Total	Administration				
		Executive	Admin.	Personnel	Secretarial	Finance & accounting
(a) Controllable costs						
Salaries and wages (as per management structure)	225,000	12,000	7,000	7,000		10,000
		3,000	9,000			12,000
			8,000			
			5,000			
			2,000			
Pension	9,000	1,000	1,000	1,000		1,000
National Insurance	6,000	500	500	500		500
Total employment costs	240,000	16,500	32,500	8,500		23,500
Energy	20,000	500	1,000	1,000	1,000	1,500
Advertising	15,000					
Telephone	6,000	500	1,000	500	1,000	1,000
Insurance	2,000		500			500
Travelling	5,000	500	1,500	500	500	
	288,000	18,000	36,500	10,500	2,500	26,500
(b) Non-controllable costs						
Rent	400,000	10,000	30,000	10,000	10,000	20,000
Rates	250,000	6,000	18,000	6,000	6,000	12,000
Insurance	5,000		5,000			
General	6,000		4,000			
Administration	10,000		7,000	1,000	1,000	1,000
Bank interest	15,000					
	686,000	16,000	64,000	17,000	17,000	33,000
Summary:						
(a) Controllable costs	288,000	18,000	36,500	10,500	2,500	26,500
(b) Non-controllable costs	686,000	16,000	64,000	17,000	17,000	33,000
	974,000	34,000	100,500	27,500	19,500	59,500
Depreciation	69,000					5,000
	1,034,000	34,000	100,500	27,500	19,500	64,500

Corporate development	Production control & maintenance	Production					Marketing, sales & despatch	Transport delivery & storage
		Cabinet shop	Speaker assembly	Cabinet assembly	Unit assembly	System assembly		
6,000	8,000	25,000	15,000	15,000	10,000	5,000	10,000	3,000
	4,000	2,000	2,000	2,000	2,000	2,000	6,000	9,000
	3,000						12,000	
							9,000	
	1,000	1,000	500	500	500		500	1,000
	500	500	500	500	500	500	500	500
6,000	16,500	28,500	18,000	18,000	13,000	7,500	38,000	13,500
		5,000	2,000	1,000	2,000	1,000	1,000	3,000
							15,000	
							2,000	
	1,000						2,000	
6,000	17,500	33,500	20,000	19,000	15,000	8,500	58,000	16,500
5,000	5,000	40,000	30,000	30,000	50,000	30,000	30,000	100,000
3,000	3,000	25,000	18,000	18,000	30,000	18,000	18,000	69,000
	2,000							
		2,000	2,000	2,000	2,000	2,000	2,000	3,000
8,000	10,000	67,000	50,000	50,000	82,000	50,000	50,000	172,000
6,000	17,500	33,500	20,000	19,000	15,000	8,500	58,000	16,500
8,000	10,000	67,000	50,000	50,000	82,000	50,000	50,000	172,000
14,000	27,500	100,500	70,000	69,000	97,000	58,500	108,000	188,500
	10,000	15,000	2,500	2,500	2,500	2,500		20,000
14,000	37,500	115,500	72,500	71,500	99,500	61,000	108,000	208,500

Leisure Sound Ltd: Profit and loss account for year ended 31 December

	1982 actual, £'000	1982 budget, £'000	1982 variance, £'000	1981 actual, £'000
Sales	2,088	2,200	(112)	1,800
Stock at 1.1.82	236	230	(6)	200
Purchases	1,024	1,035	11	711
	1,260	1,265	5	911
Deduct stock 31.12.82	498	350	(148)	236
Cost of materials	762	915	153	675
Overhead and other expenditure	974	960	(14)	940
Depreciation	60	65	5	40
Total cost of sales	1,796	1,940	144	1,655
Profit before tax	292	260	32	145
Taxation	135	125	(10)	75
Profit after tax	157	135	22	70
Dividend	50	45	(5)	40
Retained and added to reserves	107	90	17	30

Leisure Sound Ltd: Net assets at 31 December

	1982 actual, £'000	1982 budget, £'000	1981 actual, £'000
Fixed assets:			
Goodwill	120	120	120
Plant & machinery	230	250	270
Fixtures & fittings	50	45	40
Motor vehicles	100	80	80
	500	495	510
Net current assets:			
Stock	498	350	236
Trade debtors	250	235	220
Current assets	748	585	456
Trade creditors	288	240	190
Bank overdraft	102	30	80
Taxation	135	125	110
Proposed dividend	50	45	40
Current liabilities	575	440	420
	173	145	36
Net assets	673	640	546
Capital employed			
Share capital	400	400	400
Reserves	66	70	36
Retained profit	107	90	30
	173	160	66
Shareholder's funds	573	560	466
Long-term loans	100	80	80
Capital employed	673	640	546

Leisure Sound Ltd: Cash flow statement for year ended 31 December 1982

	Actual, £'000	Budget, £'000	Variance, £'000
Revenue:			
Profit before tax	292	264	28
Taxation	(110)	(110)	—
Dividend	(40)	(40)	—
Increase in net current assets			
Stock	(262)	(114)	(148)
Debtors	(30)	(15)	(15)
Creditors	98	50	48
Net inflow/(outflow)	(52)	35	(87)
Capital:			
Capital expenditure	(50)	(50)	—
Long-term loan	20	—	20
Depreciation	60	65	(5)
Net inflow	30	15	15
Bank balance			
(Net outflow)	(22)		
Net inflow		50	(72)
Bank overdraft at 1 January 1982	(80)	(80)	—
Bank overdraft at 31 December 1982	(102)	(30)	(72)

Leisure Sound Ltd: Management ratios

	1982 actual	1982 budget		1981 actual		1980 actual
Sales, £'000	2,088	2,200		1,800		1,550
Growth, £'000	288			250		
Growth, %	16			16		
Real growth (excluding inflation)	2			4		
Variance from budget, £'000	(112)					
Cost of materials	36.5%	41.6%		37.5%		38.1%
Gross profit margin	63.5%	58.4%		62.5%		61.9%
	100.0%	100.0%		100.0%		100.0%
Cost structure:						
Sales	*100%*	*100%*		*100%*		*100%*
Cost of materials	36.5	41.6		37.5		38.1
Expenses	46.6	43.7		52.2		51.3
Depreciation	2.9	2.9		2.2		1.6
Profit before tax	14.0	11.8		8.1		9.0
Capital employed (£'000):						
(year-end net assets)†	960	840		776		626
Return on capital employed	39.6%	32.5%		20.0%		24.0%
Gearing ratio: (net borrowing/ shareholders' fund + borrowing)	26.1%	16.4%		25.6%		26.9%
Total debt ratio: (total debt*/ shareholders' fund + total debt)	54.1%	48.1%		51.8%		53.2%
Current Ratio: (current assets/ current liabilities)	1.3	1.3		1.1		1.2

*Total debt consists of long-term loans and current liabilities.
†See note to Section 5.6.3.

Because of the varying trading structures, no accepted basis exists for the compilation of capital employed in terms of net assets. Two principles must be observed:

1 That the basis is consistent from period to period.
2 That the comparison is based on a like-for-like basis.

The capital employed at £775,000, being the actual year-end net assets at 31 December 1982 is calculated by adding to the net assets of £673,000 (Section 10.2) the amount of bank borrowing, £102,000 (Section 10.2). This adjustment excludes from the return on capital calculations the method used to finance the net assets employed in the business.

Correspondingly, the amount of interest payable and included in the accounts (£15,000 in the year to 31 December 1982) must be added back to the profit before tax, £292,000 (Section 10.2) to give an adjusted profit of £307,000. When related to the investment in the net assets of £775,000 a return of 39.6% is recorded.

The adequacy or otherwise of return on capital (or net assets) is a major subject and because of the wide variety of trading concerns could not be effectively covered in this book.

10.3.1 Additional management ratios

Markets:
  growth of market share
  length of order book/sales
  debtors/sales

Capital:
  net profit after tax/shareholders' funds
  interest paid/borrowed capital
  total profit/interest paid
  borrowed capital/equity capital
  earnings per share
  dividend paid/market value
  dividend paid/attributable profit

Suppliers:
  suppliers' prices index
  suppliers' lead time
  days orders overdue
  creditors/purchases
  cash, debtors, marketable securities/current liabilities
  value of goods returned or credited/purchases

Employees:
  number of leavers/average numbers employed
  average of senior staff: now/five years ago
  'output' per employee

Assets:
  net profit before tax and interest to total assets
  liquid assets/current liabilities
  actual output/maximum output

The Budget is either achieved or not.

The achievement may be better or worse than budget.

The budget was either based on an optimistic or pessimistic plan.

The company's objectives may or may not require to be amended.

The plan may have been correct but outside influences may have altered the trading environment.

The effect of these influences may not have been foreseen or if foreseen may have been quantified incorrectly.

The management information system may have monitored the deviations to allow corrective action.

The corrective action may or may not have been effective.

The management information system may have been too inflexible to monitor deviations.

The system will require overhaul before the planning process for the next year commences (see Section 10.4.3).

The lessons learned should be fed into the next year's planning.

Specific areas in which profitability and return on capital can be improved should be activated (see Sections 10.4.4 and 10.5.1).

Leisure Sound Ltd
Expenditure by function: year to 31 December 1982

£'000	Executive		Admin.		Personnel		Secretarial		Finance & accounting		Planning		Production & maintenance		Packing & selling		Despatch & storage		Total	
	Act.	Var.	Act.	Var.	Act.	Var.	Act.	Var.	Act.	Var.	Act.	Var.	Act.	Var.	Act.	Var.	Act.	Var.	Act.	Var.
Actual expenditure																				
Controllable	18	–	36	3	11	1	2	–	32	–	6	1	28	3	58	2	36	5		
Non-controllable	16	–	64	(7)	17	–	17	11	33	(17)	8	–	10	(1)	50	(1)	172	(10)		
Total direct cost	34	–	100	(4)	28	1	19	11	65	(17)	14	1	38	2	108	1	208	(5)	614	(10)
Recoverable from production departments																				
Cabinet shop	–	–	6	1	4	(1)	–	–	3	–	–	–	10	–	12	(1)	20	2		–
Speaker assembly	–	–	7	(–)	2	–	–	–	3	–	–	–	8	–	1	–	1	1		–
Cabinet assembly	–	–	13	(–)	2	2	–	–	2	(–)	–	–	6	–	15	–	10	1		–
Unit assembly	–	–	5	–	8	(5)	–	–	3	–	–	–	5	1	20	(1)	20	2		–
Systems assembly	–	–	20	(2)	3	–	–	–	5	(2)	–	–	8	–	30	–	50	–		–
Total recovery	–	–	51	(2)	19	(3)	5	–	16	(1)	–	–	37	3	77	(2)	100	5	305	–
Net direct cost	34	–	49	(2)	9	(2)	14	11	49	(16)	14	1	1	(1)	31	(1)	108	–	309	(10)

Act. = Actual
Var. = Variance from budget

Leisure Sound Ltd
Actual income and expenditure: year to 31 December 1982

Production departments	Department income			Material	Controllable direct expenditure	Gross contribution	Non-controllable expenditure		Contribution
	Sales	Transfers	Total revenue (notional)				Direct	Allocated	
Cabinet shop	24,000	144,000	168,000	112,000	48,500	7,500	67,000	56,000	(115,500)
Speaker assembly	–	240,000	240,000	96,500	22,500	121,000	50,000	21,000	50,000
Cabinet assembly	64,000	640,000	704,000	351,500	21,500	331,000	50,000	49,000	232,000
Unit assembly	100,000	720,000	1,010,000	680,500	17,500	322,000	82,000	62,000	178,000
System assembly	1,700,000	–	1,700,000	1,239,500	11,000	449,500	50,000	117,500	282,000
	2,088,000	1,744,000	3,832,000	2,480,000	121,000	1,231,000	299,000	305,500	626,500
Unrealised profit in stock									26,000
									600,500
Overheads:									
Executive					18,000		14,000	(–)	
Administration					36,500		64,000	(51,000)	
Personnel					10,500		17,000	(19,000)	
Secretarial					2,500		33,000	(5,000)	
Finance and accounting					31,500		8,000	(16,000)	
Corporate development					6,000		–	–	
Production and maintenance					27,500		10,000	(37,000)	
Packing and selling					57,000		50,000	(77,000)	
Delivery and storage					36,500		112,000	(100,000)	
Total overheads					227,000		397,000	(305,500)	308,500
Net contribution					348,000		696,000		£292,000

Allocation to production departments.
£'000

	Cabinet manuf.	Speaker assembly	Cabinet assembly	Unit assembly	Systems assembly	Total
Administration	6	7	13	5	20	51
Personnel	4	2	2	8	3	19
Secretarial	1	1	1	1	1	5
Finance and accounting	3	3	2	3	5	16
Production and maintenance	10	8	6	5	8.5	37.5
Packing and selling	12	–	15	20	30	77
Delivery and storage	20	–	10	20	50	100
	56	21	49	62	117.5	305.5

155

10.4.3 Management information systems design

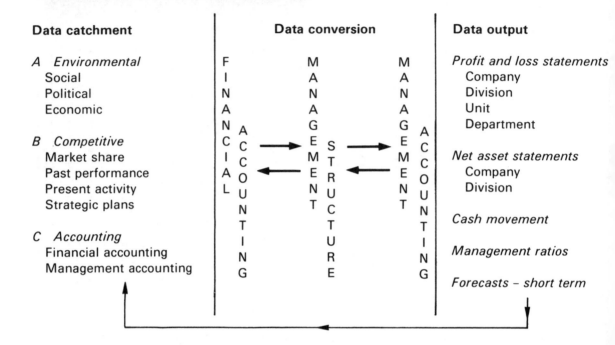

Data catchment

A *Environmental*
  Social
  Political
  Economic

B *Competitive*
  Market share
  Past performance
  Present activity
  Strategic plans

C *Accounting*
  Financial accounting
  Management accounting

Data conversion

FINANCIAL ACCOUNTING → MANAGEMENT STRUCTURE → MANAGEMENT ACCOUNTING

Data output

Profit and loss statements
  Company
  Division
  Unit
  Department

Net asset statements
  Company
  Division

Cash movement

Management ratios

Forecasts – short term

Is information presented in such a way that it assists in decision-making?

Does information indicate each responsible individual's achievements and level of required performance? Are responsibilities clearly defined?

Does the information presented enable the individual manager to make plans and set standards?

Do reports present both results and — in so far as possible — the reasons behind these results?

Are past and present levels of performance emphasised in reports?

Is the reporting structure flexible?

Are established goals and other standards stressed as benchmarks in reports?

Is information about the future given in reports?

Is information of a non-financial nature reported where it has relevance to financial outcomes?

Is information on external conditions (as they might bear on a particular organisation's operations) given in reports?

Is each report oriented towards its recipient, considering both his level and function?

Do reports give as much information as possible in quantitative terms?

Are reports suitably succinct? Is exception reporting encouraged?

Are recipients of reports urged to consider fully their content and to discuss this with colleagues and staff?

Is an appropriate and known degree of accuracy secured in reported information?

Does management realise that the study of management information and reporting systems is not necessarily concerned with computers?

Is it understood that more data in reports does not in itself mean more information for management?

Does management know that information needs cannot all be predetermined by systems studies?

Is it appreciated that for information to be instantly available does not necessarily increase its value or usefulness? And that frequent reporting does not necessarily mean that information is thereby more useful? Half-accurate information on time is better than totally correct information too late.

Is management by exception practised in designing and compiling reports?

Are reports understood?

Is unnecessary detail eliminated from reports?

Do reports call the attention of higher levels of management in those situations that cannot be controlled at lower levels?

Is each report that is produced really necessary?

Can reports be condensed, or combined one with another?

Can the frequency of issue of reports be altered?

Is an interest in the reporting system maintained at all levels of management?

Can significant figures be produced and communicated between normal reporting dates?

Are regular review meetings held to consider reports, results, and the adequacy of reporting systems?

Are attempts made to explain variations from plan in an upwards direction in the organisation before criticism proceeds downwards to the source of variation?

Are the duties and responsibilities of all those concerned with producing reports clearly defined?

Is the chart of accounts compatible with the requirements of the reporting system? Does either take precedence?

Are controllable expenses segregated from those that are non-controllable?

Are results reported in the same manner in which managers plan and think about their operations?

Are reports presented in an easy-to-read format?

Is appropriate use made of ratios and percentages?

Are figures in reports rounded whenever possible?

Is follow-up properly planned?

Can the reader grasp easily the developments from the reports, act on these or ensure other action?

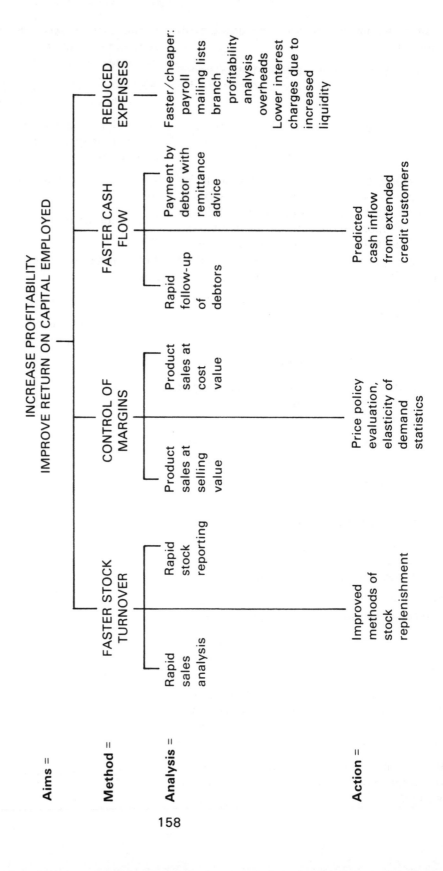

10.4.4 Appraisal of financial objectives

Aims =   INCREASE PROFITABILITY
IMPROVE RETURN ON CAPITAL EMPLOYED

Method =   FASTER STOCK TURNOVER | CONTROL OF MARGINS | FASTER CASH FLOW | REDUCED EXPENSES

Analysis =
- Rapid sales analysis
- Rapid stock reporting
- Product sales at selling value
- Product sales at cost value
- Rapid follow-up of debtors
- Payment by debtor with remittance advice
- Faster/cheaper: payroll mailing lists branch profitability analysis overheads
- Lower interest charges due to increased liquidity

Action =
- Improved methods of stock replenishment
- Price policy evaluation, elasticity of demand statistics
- Predicted cash inflow from extended credit customers

10.5 PLANNING FOR NEXT YEAR

10.5.1 Procedure for improving productivity and profitability

The planning for next year, as a basis for a budget, commences against the background of a structural approach as in Section 10.5.1 to improve productivity and profitability.

Short term

Evaluate products

↓

Detailed appraisal

↓

Set pricing policy

↓

Consider the discount policy

↓

Combat price competition
by raising or lowering prices

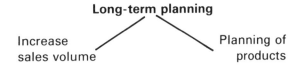

Long-term planning

Increase   Planning of
sales volume   products

Effect of product mix on profits

A company can make no more profit than its maximised product mix will allow

The practical criteria for evaluating products have reference to:
   market share
   the relevance of each product to the rest of
      the range
   the sales volume of the product
   the degree to which capital or other scarce
      resources are committed to the product,
      such as management or machine time
   the importance of the product to customers
   its vulnerability, in terms of markets,
      supplies or costs, to the impact of inflation
      or government or labour action
   sales forecasting/production planning,
      diffuculties, short runs, etc

its influence on credit, customer discounts or bad debts

its impact upon company reputation

the growth prospects in the market

its coverage of overheads

the degree to which it ties up sales or service time

its impact upon costs such as waste, breakages, sales commissions

its market acceptance

market competition

These questions will lead to other more detailed appraisals:

How much could be gained by product modification or value analysis?

How far can the price be increased dramatically or the product quality be degraded, or both, either as a prelude to abandonment or in place of it?

How much could be gained by modifying the marketing and sales strategy?

How good are the other opportunities in this product area?

How much useful management time and resource can be gained by dropping the product?

How much in total monetary revenue is the product contributing beyond its direct costs, minus any indirect costs which are incurred marketing, selling and distributing this product specifically?

How much is the sale of this product contributing to the sale of other products in this range?

Has the market got potential for the future and, if so, what?

Long-term planning of products and mix:

For long-term planning purposes the following questions need to be asked:

When is the company likely to face situations of product shortage either because of materials supply or the disruption of production?

How extensive are the situations likely to be?

How will competition attempt to reduce total demand, how do they allocate scarce products and how can the company gain a competitive or profit advantage from this?

What role is played by sales management in deciding how such situations should be handled, and is the special difficulty of the personal selling task at this time recognised?

What are the implications of government policy and special legislation which may be prompted by company policies and which would damage either the market, the supply or long-term company profitability?

Increasing sales volume:

Cutting the size of the sales force

Changing sales methods

Improving volume per order

Increasing the order- to call-ratio

Increasing price, reducing discounts

Lowering customer service levels

Concentration upon high-growth, high-profit customers

Area expansion

Reduction of customer population

Change of sales force remuneration, incentives

Identifying marginal opportunities for growth

Improving sales skills, product, or customer knowledge

Key account development

Providing sales and customer incentives

Product planning is essential, principles of which are:

To thoroughly measure the likely impact of inflation upon all key markets and products, and to pay close day-to-day attention to sudden developments.

If the operation has to be cut back, cut it back

hard though not necessarily fast, but do it earlier rather than later.

Offer a tighter, streamlined product range with contingency funds held to exploit sudden opportunities.

Develop overseas and other markets which are less prone to inflationary impact. To move from a high fixed cost manufacturing base towards a low fixed cost service organisation is one such option. Service organisations with low capital intensity seem to ride inflation rather better than manufacturing organisations.

For new product development, speculate a little, particularly into those areas which do not tie up capital or technical resources and where there is a possibility of a small but fast payback. There are many such opportunities in the market which large companies often ignore because of their small potential size. These become much more attractive in times of zero growth. An acquisition policy towards innovative but small companies may be one answer.

Invest at the point when the market is at its most depressed, when some are saying it will become even worse but the company judges it is improving. A high market share, established at the point when the market is depressed, will pay for itself handsomely when substantial volume reappears.

Pricing policy:

A pricing policy must take into account a company's freedom to act within the following framework:

Dominance of the company's market position
The degree to which substitute products are available
The likelihood of competitive response.
The anticipated rise in costs
The degree to which sales and price are related within the chosen market sector
The company's long-term business and market objective

The anticipated developments in technology
The need for company growth in sales volume
Government restrictions on price
Relatively small pricing moves which may have a dramatic impact upon profits

Discount policy:

Alongside a sound pricing policy must be a valid and effective discount policy with adequate controls, since:

Discounts may fall within pricing regulations.

It is harder to reduce a customer's discounts than increase the list price.

Buyers seek more favourable discount terms when prices go up and play off one supplier against another.

Additional discounts tend to stay in the customer's pocket rather than being passed through to the end user, hence the market size is not increased.

Short-term and promotional discounts have a tendency to become firmly established as standard discount.

Standard discounts for bulk orders or for rapid payments or for turnover volume have a tendency to be claimed, even when the conditions under which they are offered are not met.

Criteria for combating price competition:

A lower price, and make a charge for delivery or for after-sales service.

Lower prices for bulk orders delivered less frequently.

Lower prices against guaranteed orders over a period, paid in advance, or in stages.

Lower prices for sole supplier rights.

Reciprocal deals, with products and services being exchanged.

Guidelines for altering product or service prices

Upwards:
Raise prices when everyone else does.

Avoid too frequent price rises.

Provide a short moratorium on the price increase for key customers.

Provide advance notice of the price increase allowing customers to stock up at old prices.

Offer some economy at the same time – a price reduction on small selling items – a promotional short-term discount, and so on.

Make a good case for the price increase, e.g. cost increases non-controllable also demonstrate how the company's productivity or profit improvement programme has helped to absorb some of the increase.

Show customers how they can change their buying pattern to minimise the effect of the increase.

Introduce a new lower-price, lower-quality version of the product.

Offer alternative payment or service terms.

Downwards:
Cut the price when the competition is quiet, or preferably when they are raising their prices.

Make the price cut deep enough. It has to be deep enough to overcome the normal inertia of the market and to 'pay' a buyer for his trouble in considering a new supplier.

Do it without notice and promote it very widely. Be careful not to stock load large customers beforehand.

Do it only when the price cut can be sustained for a long time, preferably when competition will have great difficulty in meeting it.

Never do it unless the market is demonstrably price sensitive.

Never do it as a crisis measure when profits are low and the market is turning down, competitors will copy to survive, and a price or discount war will result.

Do it on selected loss-leading lines, with other products trailed at normal prices.

Monitor situations:

Cost controls exist to ensure that actual costs correspond to planned costs. Information and action are central to effective cost control.

Cost control is quite a different activity to cost reduction and the two must not be confused.

162

Management aids to assist in the planning and budgeting process based on trading and financial data for the 1982 year are given in the following sections:

10.6.1   Break-even graph
10.6.2   Seasonal pattern of sales
10.6.3   Total sales and moving annual total
10.6.4   Trade debtors

Consideration will be given to incorporating these aids in the management reporting system for 1983.

(please see overleaf for graph)

Checklist

Is this presentation part of the management accounting procedure or supplementary to it?

Should the budget break-even be presented with the budget financial information?

Does the graph add to the decision-taking process?

Based upon an effective 90% of capacity, is a 66% level of production unacceptably high before profits are earned?

How effectively can fixed or variable costs be cut or modified?

Does the graph highlight aspects of the information not easily recognised from other accounting information?

Does it highlight the critical aspect of capacity utilisation?

Is the information too general when related to total company performance?

Should supplementary graphs be prepared for each main activity?

How could this be achieved with large volumes of interdepartmental sales?

Are there too many variables to be taken into account for regular presentation of the graphs?

Should representation be related to forecast information?

Could the level of capacity utilisation be regularly reviewed and incorporated within the company's objectives?

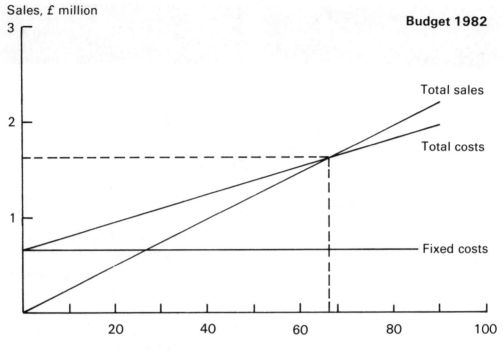

Sales, £ million

Budget 1982

Total sales

Total costs

Fixed costs

Percentage of total manufacturing and assembly capacity

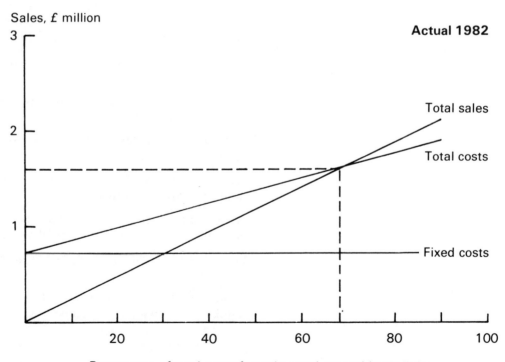

Sales, £ million

Actual 1982

Total sales

Total costs

Fixed costs

Percentage of total manufacturing and assembly capacity

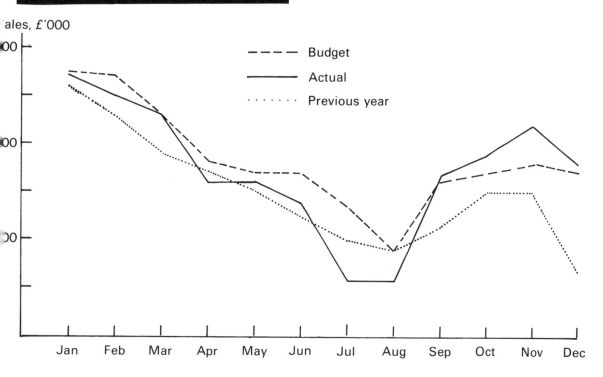

10.6.2 Seasonal pattern of sales and checklist

Sales, £'000

Budget
Actual
Previous year

Jan Feb Mar Apr May Jun Jul Aug Sep Oct Nov Dec

Checklist

Does this graph convey comparative informa-tion in a recognisable form?

Should a graph be incorporated into the management accounting procedures?

What information is considered essential for presentation on the graph?

Can too much information be incorporated to the point of confusion?

Are the scales used on the graph acceptable?

Could they distort the interpretation of the facts?

What is the reason for the peaks and troughs in the sales year?

Is there evidence of similarity between years?

Is this pattern convenient for production, financing, stock piling, etc?

Could this seasonal pattern be a disadvantage to effective company control and performance?

What marketing effort should be introduced to attempt to alter the seasonality of the sales?

Should efforts be made to introduce new lines of sales which have the opposite seasonal patterns to level out income from sales?

What is the reason for a deeper trough in sales income in 1982 than anticipated?

Why was the selling peak in November higher than anticipated?

Were external factors interplaying upon the company?

Were these external factors national or competitive?

To whom should graphs containing this information be sent for comment?

Checklist

Does this graph provide sufficient information about sales trends to allow prompt corrective action by management?

Does the trend when highlighted impact on other functions or departments, e.g. production, distribution and finance?

Should the graphical presentation be a part of the normal managing process?

Is a presentation of this kind more revealing than lists of data?

What period should be covered by the graph?

Should a supplementary graph cover past and projected presentation?

Is the result confusing?

To whom or which function should this information be available?

Should probable results be forecast and the trend lines be incorporated on the graph?

What is the effect of inflation upon the sales trend?

Is the company's sales growth real or apparent?

How does growth match the company's objectives?

Can the information be used in sales training courses?

What positive action should be taken to alleviate the percentage variances?

What is the permitted percentage variance before major action?

Is it accepted that the 'Moving Total' indicates trend by eliminating seasonal aspects of sales?

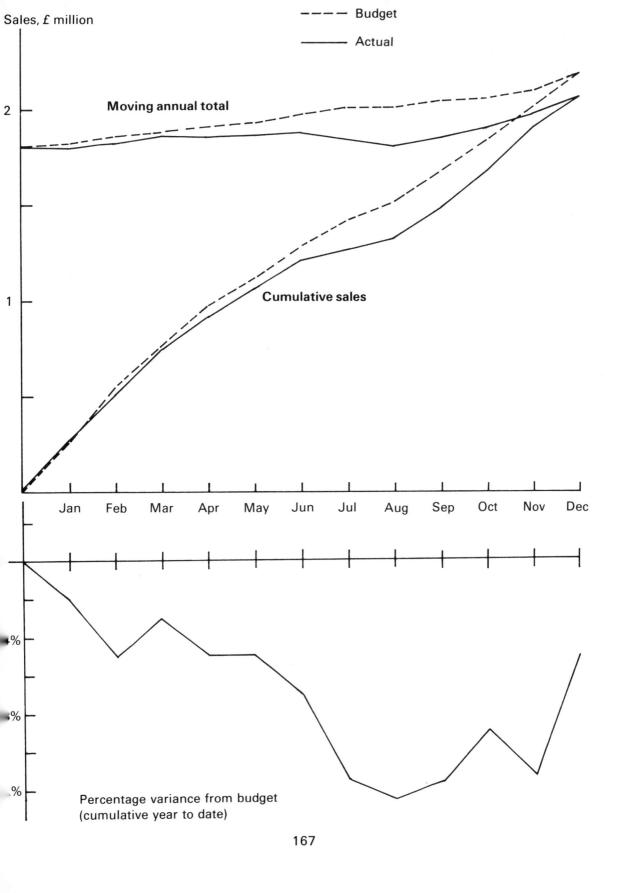

Sales, £ million

Budget
Actual

Moving annual total

Cumulative sales

Jan Feb Mar Apr May Jun Jul Aug Sep Oct Nov Dec

Percentage variance from budget
(cumulative year to date)

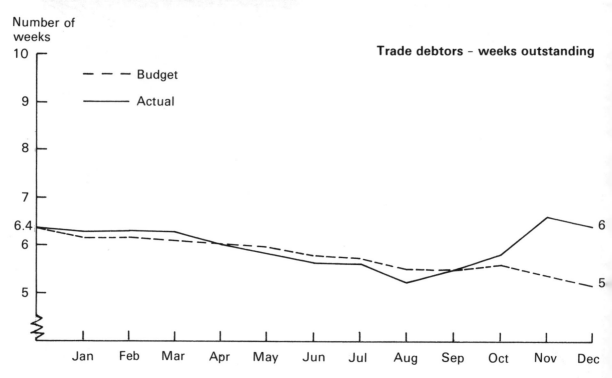

Trade debtors – weeks outstanding

Checklist

Have the questions raised in the seasonal pattern of sales graph (Section 10.6.2) any bearing on the trend of debtors as shown in this graph?

Is the number of weeks' credit outstanding generally acceptable?

Are competitive companies' debtors running at about this level?

Can the company afford to allow credit at this level?

Have comments been raised by the banks regarding the number of weeks outstanding?

Why does the trend in outstanding debtors not follow the seasonal pattern of sales more closely?

Can different payment terms be introduced to shorten the outstanding number of weeks?

Could this have an adverse effect on sales?

Who would introduce the revised policy: sales force or accounts?

Which function is responsible for collecting outstanding accounts?

Does this cause customer liaison problems?

Why did the credit outstanding suddenly rise from October?

Was the budget wrong or was it external reaction; restriction of money supply by banks?

Considering the increasing turnover, is it credible to hold the number of weeks' credit at the same as the previous year?

Could it be that the previous year was too high because of ineffective credit control?

How to present management information efficiently

As was mentioned in Unit 2, there is no right or wrong way to structure or control an enterprise; the market, location, structure and management team are all variable factors. The style of management as laid down by those individuals in senior positions has a direct bearing on the manner in which the enterprise will be run.

This style invariably predetermines the type and amount of output from the information system. The balance of too much against too little is a constant challenge to management.

Information requirements should be regularly examined to ensure that the needs at all levels of management are satisfied. The pressures acting on the enterprise, both from outside and from within, necessitate a review of its practices. Information retrieval and presentation is an important part of that review.

There are many ways to say the same thing and there are many ways to present trading and financial information. The important aspect is that management must receive the information which it needs to manage.

The foregoing Units contain examples of data presentation, be they in tabular form or in graphical form. This Unit contains further examples of data presentation, again tabular or graphical, to stimulate the thinking of the reader. Personal choice and style cannot be overlooked.

Contents of Unit 3

3 'Easy reference' information in graphical format

Checklist for management information reporting

Plain language:
    Accepted method of communication
    Clarity necessitates length of explanation
    Difficulty in use of alphanumeric characters
    Salient facts obscure
    Inflexibility
    Stimulation of reader's interest

Forms:
    Tabular presentation in everyday use
    Characters segregated
    Facts displayed simply
    Avoidance of confusion
    Constant opportunity to review layout and clarity
    Permits regular challenge of essential information
    Minimum of plain-language explanation
    Volume of paper restricted
    Restricted cost of production

Graphs:
    Enables comparisons
    Timescales unrestricted
    Trend identification
    Allows easy assimilation of salient facts
    Condenses information volumes
    Assists forecasting

1 Management control information

Examples of presentation of management control information essential for the day-to-day control of a business and its future.

Department:

Time period covered:

Plan		Performance			Corrective action	Year to date				Anticipated result for year		
Job item	Target this month	Results this month	Variance	Variances ranked by significance		*Cumulative* target	results	variances	Diary, i.e. explanation of past variances	Target for year	Latest anticipated result for year	Variances, i.e. forecast for whole year (past & future)

Total quality-cost estimate (12 months equivalent)

Company: Division:		Date: Dept. Unit:		
	Item	£'000	Total, %	Turn- over, %
Internal failure;	1 Scrap 2 Rework 3 Repair 4 Excess operation time 5 Excess production 6 Corrective operations 7 Tooling revision 8 Give away 9 Trouble shooting 10 Design changes 11 Down grading			
External failure:	1 Warranty 2 Customer service 3 Customer returns			
Appraisal:	1 Purchase acceptance 2 In process acceptance 3 Outgoing product approval 4 Quality inf. equipment 5 Inspection mfg. tools 6 Reliability monitoring 7 Quality audits 8 Training 9 Quality records 10 Outside appraisal services 11 Customer liaison			

Prevention:	1 Design quality
	     improvement
	2 Vendor quality
	     improvement
	3 Plan product/process
	     controls
	4 Plan acceptable jobs
	5 Conformance quality
	     improvement
	6 Eval. customer satisfaction
	7 Quality education
	8 Executive quality reporting			

Total			100	
Turnover				100

DISTRIBUTION COST CONTROL FORM

Location:	Month:					
	Budget			*Actual*		
Activity	*Activity level*	*Cost*	*Unit cost*	*Activity level*	*Cost*	*Unit cost*
Warehousing: Fixed charges Pallets Lighting Maintenance Miscellaneous						
TOTAL						
Handling: Fixed charges Power Equipment repairs Salaries Wages, overtime Miscellaneous						
TOTAL						
Distribution: Fixed charges Wages, overtime Vehicle repairs Tyres Fuel and oil Vehicle hire Miscellaneous						
TOTAL						
Administration: Fixed charges Salaries overtime Telephones Postages Lighting and heating Miscellaneous						
TOTAL						

Overdue orders at 6 a.m. Monday

Issued by Production Planning

Date of issue:

Works order	Customer	Location	Quoted availability	Quantity pack	Product	Production unit stage	Respon-sibility	Reason	Action proposed comments

178

Data sheet 5
DAILY CONTRIBUTION CONTROL REPORT

Daily contribution report
Period:

Date:
Day:

Machine number	Comparison against target				Job		Comparison against job standard						Number of shifts on job
	Contribution, £				Product ref.	Description	Production, units		Contribution, £				
	Daily performance						Actual	Std/day	Daily performance				
	Cum. var.	Var.	Target	Actual					Actual	Std	Var.	Cum. var.	
1	3,000	50	350	400	1	Transistor	80	80	400	400	—	—	1
2	—	50	200	250	1,387	Electronic valve	125	100	250	200	50	500	12
3	(1,000)	(275)	500	225	86	VHF tuner	75	100	225	300	(75)	(500)	6

TOTAL SALES REPORT

Total sales report, 4 months, 1982

	Units, '000s		Price, £		Gross sales, £'000s	
	Actual	Budget	Actual	Budget	Actual	Budget
Building Products Division:						
Roof insulation	42,670	44,800	64.00	64.00	2,731	2,867
Sheathing	67,570	75,350	66.00	66.00	4,460	4,973
Tile	5,640	6,100	75.00	75.00	423	457
Plank	11,470	12,200	70.00	70.00	803	854
Wallboard	16,780	18,150	65.00	65.00	1,091	1,180
Foundation board	20,710	22,400	59.00	59.00	1,222	1,322
Form board	22,600	24,450	58.00	58.00	1,311	1,418
TOTAL	187,440	203,450			12,041	13,071
Acoustical Division:						
Tile	120,110	122,100	91.00	95.00	10,930	11,600
Board	56,050	34,880	86.00	86.00	4,820	3,000
TOTAL	176,160	156,980			15,750	14,600
Industrial Specialities Division*:						
Automotive	127,250		73.57		9,362	8,000
Refrigeration	116,530		52.06		6,066	11,000
Transportation	78,400		50.00		3,920	4,000
Other	16,000		51.00		816	1,000
TOTAL	338,180				20,164	24,000
TOTAL COMPANY	701,780				47,955	51,671

*Units not budgeted.

FLEXIBLE BUDGETARY WORK SHEET AND PERFORMANCE CONTROL

Flexible budgetary work sheet, £'000

	Budget	Volume variance	Allowed	Actual	Variance	Description
Sales	10,800	(2,400)	8,400	9,100	700	Sales price
Variable costs:						
Materials	5,000	500	4,500	4,950	(450)	Material price/usage
Other	3,000	300	2,700	2,800	(100)	Expense (variable)
Stock (increase)	(800)	800	1,600	1,600	—	
Total	7,200	1,600	5,600	6,150		
Contribution	3,600	(800)	2,800	2,950		
Fixed costs	(2,000)	—	(2,000)	2,150	(150)	Expense (fixed)
Ditto, in stock increase	200	—	200	400	200	Overheads suspended
Profit	1,800	(800)	1,000	1,200	200	

Performance summary, £

Current period				Year-to-date		
Actual	Plan	Variance		Actual	Plan	Variance
2,900	3,200	(300)	Gross sales	9,500	10,000	(500)
60	20	(40)	Discounts, etc.	100	150	50
2,840	3,180	(340)	Net sales	9,400	9,850	(450)
980	975	(5)	Standard product cost	2,450	2,500	50
1,860	2,205	(345)	Gross margin	6,950	7,350	(400)
			Manufacturing costs:			
25	10	(15)	Volume variable		60	60
275	250	(25)	Production	770	775	5
330	300	(30)	Plant overhead	830	825	(5)
15	5	(10)	Material price differences	20	10	(10)
	5	5	Other expenses	15	15	
1,215	1,635	(420)	Plant operating profits	5,315	5,665	(350)
			Administration costs:			
210	200	(10)	Distribution	675	650	(25)
260	255	(5)	Marketing	760	775	15
190	195	5	Executive	800	800	
80	60	(20)	Other (income)/expense	(150)	(50)	100
475	925	(450)	Operating profit	3,230	3,490	(260)
228	444	216	Income tax	1,550	1,675	125
247	481	(234)	Net income	1,680	1,815	(135)

Data sheet 8
CONSOLIDATED CONTROL STATEMENT

Value (£'000): Volume (units):	Quarter: Actual		Variance from budget		Year: Revisions	
0		%		%		%
Home sales (volume) Export sales (volume)						
Total sales volume		100		100		100
1.1 Home sales (gross) 1.2 Export sales (gross)						
1.0 Total sales value		100		100		100
2.0 Cost of goods						
3.0 Gross profit (1 – 2)						
4.1 Sales administration 4.2 Promotion 4.3 Service 4.4 Distribution						
4.0 Total selling expenses						
5.0 R&D costs						
6.1 Divisional HQ 6.2 Function M 6.3 Function N, etc.						
6.0 Divisional HQ and function costs						
7.0 Profit, divisional						
8.1 Company HQ 8.2 Purchasing function 8.3 Central R&D 8.4 Personnel function 8.5 Finance function, etc.						
8.0 Company HQ and function costs						
9.0 Company profit before interest and taxes						
10.0 Interest						
11.0 Taxes						
12.0 Net profit after interest and taxes						
13.0 Depreciation (2, 4, 5, 6 and 8)						
14.0 Cash flow (12 and 13)						
15.0 Dividends						
16.0 Cash flow after dividends						

17.0 Capital used: Fixed
                Current
                Total						

18.0 ROI (9:17), %						
19.0 Sales/capital (1:17), %						
20.0 Market share, %						

CONTRIBUTION EXPECTATION

Contribution expectation (£'000): four possible channels and the expected results

	Through exclusive national distributor		Through wholesaler		Through branch sales offices direct to retailers	Through branch sales offices direct to consumers
Sales to ultimate market (consumer)		700		800	900	1000
Retailers' margin	280		320		360	—
Wholesalers' margin	140		160		—	—
Distributors' margin	70				—	—
Total middlemen's margin		490		480	360	0
Manufacturer's gross sales		210		320	540	1000
Branch sales office total (inc. sales expense, physical distribution, etc.)	—		—		216	600
	—		—		—	—
Manufacturer's sales revenue deducting Branch sales office costs		210		320	324	400
Head office distribution costs:						
Advertising expense	0		48		32	20
Selling expense	0		60		—	—
Physical distribution expense (storage, assembly, packing, shipping)	21		64		48	60
Administration expenses (accounting credit, etc.)	0.2		1		0.3	0.8
Total distribution costs	21.2		173		80.3	80.8
Cost of goods sold	84		128		130	160
Total costs of distributon of goods		105.2		301	210.3	240.8
Contribution (or loss) to profit and overhead		104.8		19	113.7	159.2

Data sheet 10
RATING OF FUTURE POTENTIAL OF A NEW PRODUCT

Future expectations for the product	*Rating (R), %*											*Weight (W), %*	*Weighted rating (WR), %*
£'000	Low										High		
	0	10	20	30	40	50	60	70	80	90	100		
Market potential that can be realised												30	
Required amount of promotional expense												30	
Profit per unit												20	
Contribution to sales of other products												10	
Other contributions to firm's over-all programme												10	
TOTAL												100	

184

**CONVERSION OF NEW
PRODUCT RATING TO VOLUME**

Procedure	Product number							Total
	101	102	103	104	105	106	107	
Rating of product, %	40	80	50	80	60	20	70	400
(a) Preference ratio = $\frac{\text{Product rating, \%}}{\text{Total of ratings, \%}}$	0.10	0.20	0.125	0.20	0.15	0.05	0.175	1.0
(b) Total sales expected for next period, £								10.000
(c) Product sales expected, £ (a) x (b)	1.000	2.000	1.250	2.000	1.500	500	1.750	10.000
High expectation, £1.20 x (c)	1.200	2.400	1.500	2.400	1.800	600	2.100	12.000

This form aids management in transforming the ratings into values for expected sales volume. This procedure is primarily useful for evaluating anticipated sales of new product to be added to the product line. It may be found that some items with relatively low potential (such as product 106) are best eliminated or replaced by others.

PRODUCT EXPERIENCE AND FORECAST

Categories determining value of product	Unit of measurement	Past years			Current year	Forecast years		
		3	2	1		1	2	3
Price per unit	£							
Sales volume	No. of units							
Sales volume	No. of units							
Variable margin per unit	£							
Variable margin per year	£							
Net profit per unit	£							
Net profit per year	£							
Market share	%							
Sales as percentage of firm's total volume	%							

This form can be used for forecasting sales volume, profit, and market share of a product. Data for past years and for the current year serve as a guide to evaluating future expectations. The form is completed by sales personnel.

Estimates by several individuals may be pooled, usually by averaging, to obtain a composite set of expectations regarding prices, profits, and markets.

SALES PLANNING ANNUAL TOTALS YEARS 1 TO 5

Company:
Business Division:
Sub-business:

Notes:
1 Value in £'000
2 Volume in units

Budget of sales or profits, or market size or share

Total sales or profits, etc. by divisions, or sub-businesses, or product groups

		19X2	19X3		19X4		19X5			19X5	
		Value	Volume	Value	Volume	Value	Volume	Value	%	% Value	% Volume
A	Existing										
	New										
	Total										
B	Existing										
	New										
	Total										
C	Existing										
	New										
	Total										
D, etc.	Existing										
	New										
	Total										
Export	Existing										
	New										
	Total										
Total	Existing										
	New										
TOTALS											

This form is used to show the following, with the appropriate sub-headings above:

Planned sales by value and volume or market size by value and volume

Planned profit by value and % on sales volume

Market shares by % value and % volume

SUMMARY OF CAPITAL EMPLOYED	Company:								All values in £'000	
Balance sheet items	–4	–3	–2	–1	Plan- ning year	1	2	3	4	5
Assets:										
trade debtors	22	26	26	30	32	32	34	37	41	45
inventories	27	28	30	30	31	27	27	26	28	29
other current assets	4	3	3	2	1	2	3	1	1	1
Total current assets	53	57	59	62	64	62	64	64	70	75
Fixed assets others	35	38	40	41	42	38	39	38	40	42
Total long-term assets	35	38	40	41	42	38	39	38	40	42
Total assets	88	95	99	103	106	99	103	102	110	117
Liabilities: banks others — —										
Total current liabilities	38.0	42.2	47.4	50.9	55.2	46.0	40.5	49.6	41.7	51.7
Share capital	50	50	50	50	50	50	50	50	60	60
Reserves and retentions	—	2.8	1.6	2.1	0.8	3.0	12.5	2.4	8.3	5.3
Total liabilities	88	95	99	103	106	99	103	102	110	117

BUDGET FIXED ASSETS	Company: Business Division: Function: Company others:					All values in £'000s	
Division, functions, etc.	-1	Plan-ning year	1	2	3	4	5
Business div. A Land Buildings Equipment Others TOTAL							
Business div. B (etc.) Land Buildings Equipment Others TOTAL							
Function A Land Buildings Equipment Others TOTAL							
Function B (etc.) Land Buildings Equipment Others TOTAL							
Land Buildings Equipment Others TOTAL							
Company totals: Land Buildings Equipment Others TOTAL							

Notes:
1 Shared resources are proportionated.
2 Unallocatable assets are shown under others

Data sheet 16
PROJECTED CAPITAL EXPENDITURE

CAPITAL EXPENDITURE PROJECTS | *Company:* / *Business Division:* / *Function:*

Note:
1 All values in £ million
2 Bar lines show project time scale

Ref.	Project description and location, objective, etc.	Planning year and schedule					Project total	Analysis of total			
		1	2	3	4	5		Land	Buildings	Plant, etc.	Misc.
1	Plant installation in existing building on Site B. Increase of capacity by 500 units p.a. Objective No. 2. hydraulic transmission		0.3	0.1			0.4	—	—	0.4	—
2	Building and plant installation on Site B. Increase of capacity by 500 units p.a. Objective No. 3 hydraulic transmission				0.4	0.1	0.5	—	0.1	0.4	—
3	Acquisition of ABC Co. Ltd, London. Capacity of 100 pneumatic transmission units p.a. Market value £5m. Objective No. 4.		2.0				2.0	0.3	0.3	0.9	0.5
4, 5 etc.											
M	Minor capital projects	0.1	0.2	0.1	0.2	0.1	0.7	—	—	—	0.7
T	Totals	0.1	2.5	0.2	0.6	0.2	3.6	0.3	0.4	1.7	1.2

CAPITAL PROJECTS: PLANNING PRODUCTION CAPACITY

SUMMARY OF USE OF PRODUCTION CAPACITY	Company, business division or function: Site, building or product group:

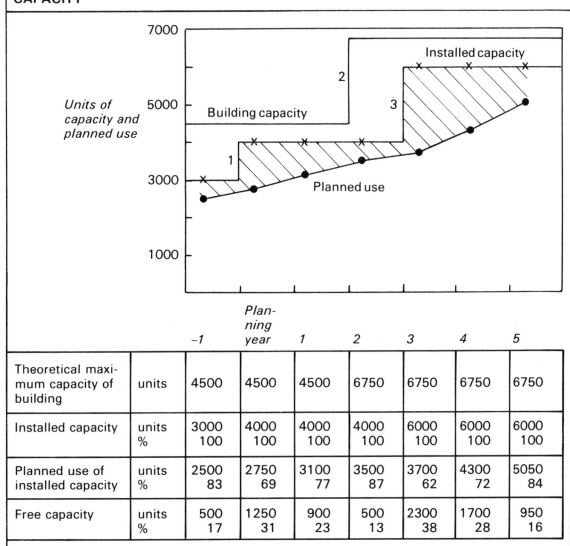

Units of capacity and planned use

Building capacity — Installed capacity — Planned use

		-1	Plan-ning year	1	2	3	4	5
Theoretical maximum capacity of building	units	4500	4500	4500	6750	6750	6750	6750
Installed capacity	units %	3000 100	4000 100	4000 100	4000 100	6000 100	6000 100	6000 100
Planned use of installed capacity	units %	2500 83	2750 69	3100 77	3500 87	3700 62	4300 72	5050 84
Free capacity	units %	500 17	1250 31	900 23	500 13	2300 38	1700 28	950 16

Notes:
1 An increase of installed capacity became effective in January of the planning year.
2 Capital expenditure, for an increase in building capacity of 50%, effective during planning year 2
3 Capital expenditure, for an increase in installed capacity of 50%, effective January of planning year 3.
4 Etc.

BUDGET CURRENT ASSETS	Company: Business Division: Function: Company HQ and others:					All values in £'000. Weeks shown as (x), etc.	
Division, function, etc.	–1	Plan-ning year	1	2	3	4	5

Business div. A
  Receivables [Debtors]
  Raw material stocks
  Finished goods
  Other
    TOTAL
	50 (x)
	20 (y)
	25 (y)
	5
	100						

Business div. B (etc.)
  Receivables
  RM stocks
  Finished goods
  Others
    TOTAL							

Function A
  Receivables
  RM stocks
  Finished goods
  Others
    TOTAL							

Function B (etc.)
  Receivables
  RM stocks
  Finished goods
  Others
    TOTAL							

Receivables RM stocks Finished goods Others TOTAL							

Company totals
  Receivables
  RM stocks
  Finished goods
  Others
    TOTAL							

Notes:
1 Functions may not need this summary.
2 Annual totals correspond with the current assets from a summary of assets.
3 The number of weeks covered is shown in brackets and is included wherever applicable.

2 Cash control information

This section gives examples of cash control information essential for the financial viability of business and future cash requirements.

Cash flow forecast (period   to   )

	Current Period	Period 1	Period 2	Period 3	Period 4	Period 5
Cash: immediately available on deposit						
Total first day of period						
Add: Net proceeds of sales Other income/receipts Working capital: increase in creditors decrease in debtors Special debtors/accounts Disposal of assets Additional funds (loan/share capital)						
Total inflow						
Deduct: Trading expenditure (by major classification) Capital expenditure Taxation Interest/dividends Special creditors/accounts Working capital: decrease in creditors increase in debtors Repayment loan/share capital						
Total outflow						
Forecast position last day of period						

REVENUE AND EXPENDITURE FORECAST

Revenue and expenditure forecast

	Current year	Year 1	Year 2	Year 3	Year 4	Year 5
Sales revenue (By major activity)						
Total sales revenue						
Operating/trading expenditure (by major classification) Fixed						
Sub-total						
Variable						
Total expenditure						
Operating/trading profit *Add:* Interest, dividends, etc. *(Deduct):* Finance charges Taxation Distributions Interest Dividends						
Retained profit						
Retained profit cumulative						
Return on average net assets						
Other financial ratios						

Accounts receivable as weeks of sales

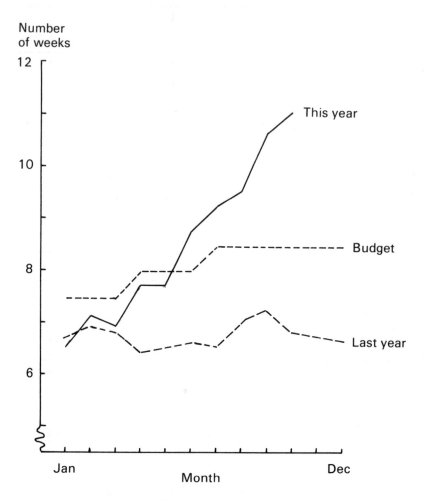

Note: The term *receivable* relates to items of working capital directly connected with the trade, e.g. debtors.

Data sheet 22
FINANCING PLAN

Financing plan

	19X0	*19X1*	*19X2*	*19X3*	*19X4*	*19X5*
Financing required (cumulative)	72.0	92.0	85.0	61.0	54.0	30.0
Financing provided (cumulative):						
Equity capital	—	—	—	—	—	—
Long-term debt	50.0	70.0	70.0	60.0	50.0	30.0
Short-term debt	22.0	22.0	15.0	1.0	4.0	—
Total financing provided	72.0	92.0	85.0	61.0	54.0	30.0

Year-end capital structure projection

	Past year	*19X0*	*19X1*	*19X2*	*19X3*	*19X4*	*19X5*
Stockholder's equity	400.0	410.0	425.0	450.0	480.0	513.0	549.0
Long-term debt	200.0	200.0	200.0	180.0	150.0	100.0	60.0
Total capital	600.0	610.0	625.0	630.0	630.0	613.0	609.0
Debt ratio*	33.3%	32.8%	32.0%	28.6%	23.8%	16.3%	9.9%
Remaining debt capacity at 25% target debt ratio	—	—	—	—	10.0	71.0	123.0

*Occasionally expressed as 'gearing ratio'.

INFORMATION BASE FOR FINANCIAL RESOURCES

INFORMATION BASE FINANCIAL RESOURCES	Company: Year:		*Note:* All sums in £'000. A is actually and P is potentially available
Resource		*Actually available*	*Potentially available*
1 Unissued Ordinary share captial	P		
2 Partially paid up but issued shares	P		
3 New share issues	P		
4 Depreciation account (if the assets represented by it are separately identifiable)	A		
5 Cash	A		
6 Marketable securities	A		
7 Extension of credit from suppliers	P		
8 Reduction of credit to customers (early settlement discounts, etc.)	P		
9 Current and planned profits	P		
10 Investment grants	P		
11 Surplus stock	A		
12 Surplus fixed assets	P		
13 Sale and lease back projects for offices, transport, equipment, etc.	P		
14 Sale of know-how	P		
Borrowing potential — the appropriate ratio based on the current value of the company's assets in land, buildings, etc., stocks and other current assets			
15 Bank overdrafts	P		
16 Long-term loans, debentures, etc.	P		
17 Discounting of bills	P		
18 Mortgages	P		
Comments:			

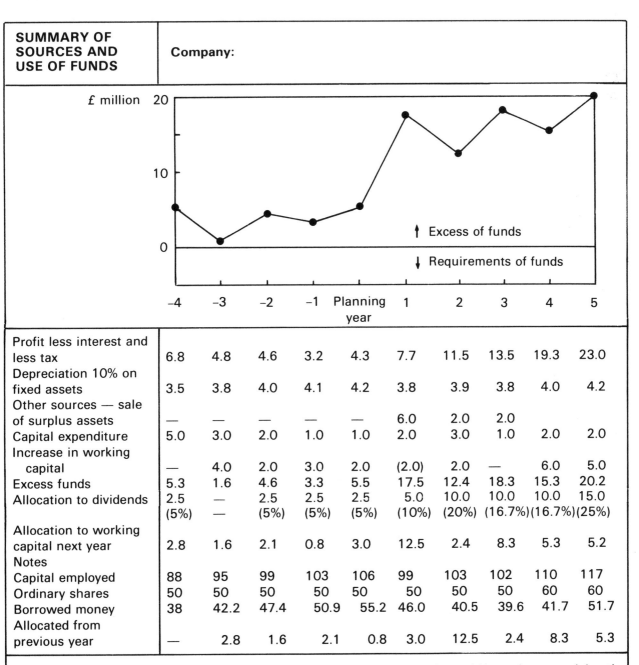

Data sheet 24										
SUMMARY OF SOURCES AND USE OF FUNDS										

SUMMARY OF SOURCES AND USE OF FUNDS	Company:									

£ million chart (see figure): Excess of funds / Requirements of funds, years −4 to 5 (Planning year)

	−4	−3	−2	−1	Planning year	1	2	3	4	5
Profit less interest and less tax	6.8	4.8	4.6	3.2	4.3	7.7	11.5	13.5	19.3	23.0
Depreciation 10% on fixed assets	3.5	3.8	4.0	4.1	4.2	3.8	3.9	3.8	4.0	4.2
Other sources — sale of surplus assets	—	—	—	—	—	6.0	2.0	2.0		
Capital expenditure	5.0	3.0	2.0	1.0	1.0	2.0	3.0	1.0	2.0	2.0
Increase in working capital	—	4.0	2.0	3.0	2.0	(2.0)	2.0	—	6.0	5.0
Excess funds	5.3	1.6	4.6	3.3	5.5	17.5	12.4	18.3	15.3	20.2
Allocation to dividends	2.5	—	2.5	2.5	2.5	5.0	10.0	10.0	10.0	15.0
	(5%)	—	(5%)	(5%)	(5%)	(10%)	(20%)	(16.7%)	(16.7%)	(25%)
Allocation to working capital next year	2.8	1.6	2.1	0.8	3.0	12.5	2.4	8.3	5.3	5.2
Notes										
Capital employed	88	95	99	103	106	99	103	102	110	117
Ordinary shares	50	50	50	50	50	50	50	50	60	60
Borrowed money	38	42.2	47.4	50.9	55.2	46.0	40.5	39.6	41.7	51.7
Allocated from previous year	—	2.8	1.6	2.1	0.8	3.0	12.5	2.4	8.3	5.3

Note: In this summary it is assumed that the tax charged is the same as that paid in each year and that the amount due to creditors remains approx. constant.

199

Cash flow from operations and capital transactions

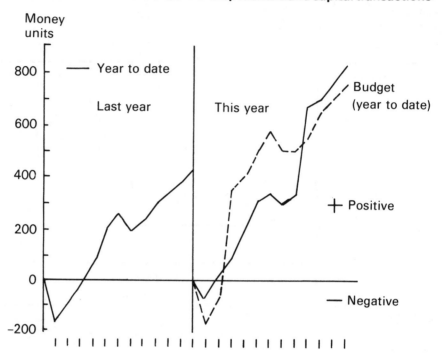

Variances (year to date)

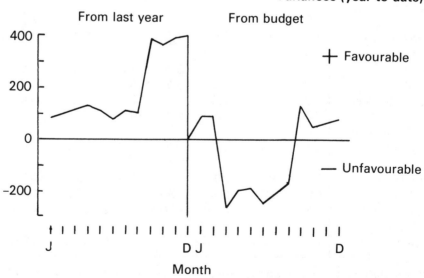

Capital expenditure forecast (period   to   ), £'000

Description	Project * A R	Cost	In-curred prior to 19X1	Incidence of future expenditure				
				19X1	19X2	19X3	19X4	19X5
1 Projects in progress 2 New projects								
Total								
3 Less disposals†	Sale price	Book value						
Total								
4 Net capital expenditure								
5 Amortisation/depreciation								

*A — additional; R — replacement
†Incidence of proceeds from disposals to be entered in forecast years

3 'Easy reference' information in graphical format

This section gives examples of 'easy reference' management information in graphical format.

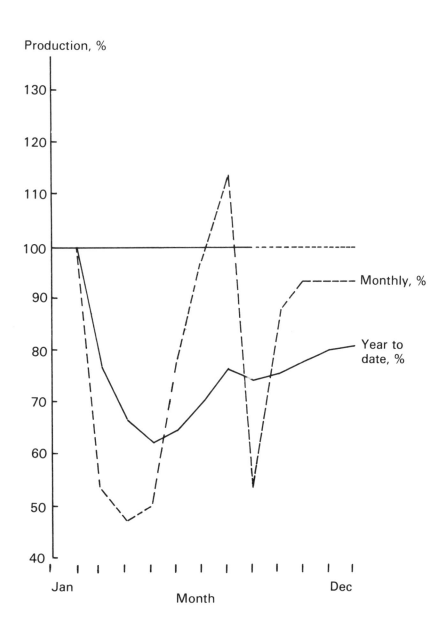

Data sheet 27
PRODUCTION AS PERCENTAGE OF NOMINAL CAPACITY

Production, %

Month

Monthly, %

Year to date, %

Jan

Dec

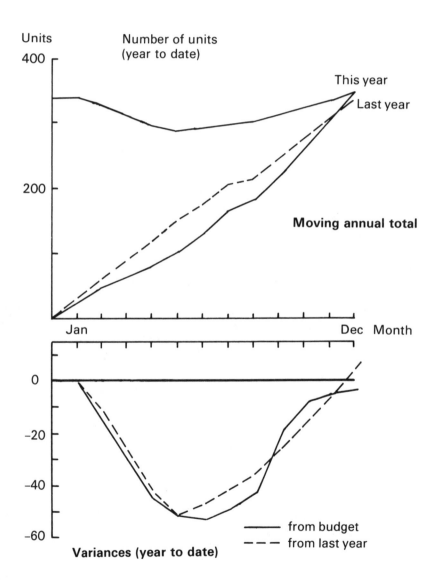

Data sheet 28
PRODUCTION TREND AND VARIANCES

Units
400

Number of units
(year to date)

This year
Last year

200

Moving annual total

Jan   Dec Month

0

−20

−40

from budget
from last year

−60

Variances (year to date)

204

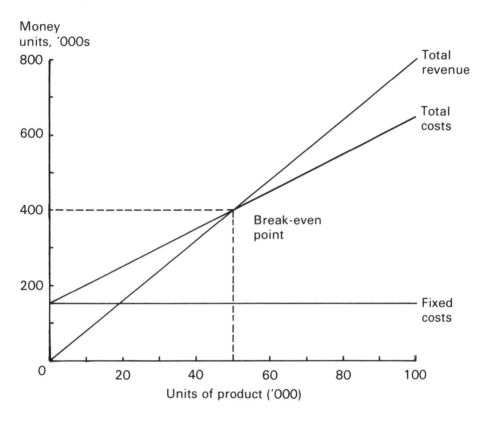

This is a graphic depiction of the break-even point computed in units of product for the single-product firm. Units of product are measured on the horizontal axis, and value (both revenues and costs) on the vertical axis. Fixed costs are shown as a constant amount, 150,000 money units at all levels of operation. Variable costs are then plotted over and above total fixed costs. The resultant line is the total cost line, including both variable and fixed costs. There is no variable cost line in the graph; variable costs are depicted as the vertical distance between the fixed cost and the total cost lines. The total cost at any point is the sum of the fixed costs plus the variable cost per unit of product multiplied by the number of units sold at that point. Total revenue at any point is the product of the unit price and the number of units sold. The upper limits of the graph are determined on the basis of the firm's full capacity, 100,000 units of product in this illustration.

Total sales, actual and cumulative, and moving annual total (MAT)

The following table sets out financial data relating to sales: total, home and export together with the trends of those sales. Data sheets 30, 31 and 32 portray the same information but in graphic format in order to assist the individual to determine a preference.

	Total sales, £'000, from Data sheet 30			Home sales, £'000, from Data sheet 31			Export sales, £'000, from Data sheet 32		
	Act.	Cum.	MAT	Act.	Cum.	MAT	Act.	Cum.	MAT
Jan	21	21	275	10	10	141	11	11	134
Feb	29	50	287	10	20	140	19	30	147
Mar	25	75	294	9	29	137	16	46	157
Apr	28	103	307	9	38	138	19	65	169
May	32	135	307	12	50	132	20	85	175
Jun	20	155	309	5	55	125	15	100	184
July	41	196	315	5	60	119	36	136	196
Aug	17	213	314	8	68	116	9	145	198
Sep	32	245	315	7	75	110	25	170	205
Oct	29	274	323	7	82	104	22	192	219
Nov	27	301	322	7	89	101	20	212	221
Dec	26	327	327	5	94	94	21	233	233
	327			94			233		

How meaningful are figures presented in the above table?

What is the significance of comparison of actual sales with moving trend of sales?

How relative is the reduction in sales to the home market compared with growth in export sales?

Does a seasonal pattern of sales emerge readily from the above data?

If not, can the information be presented in a different format?

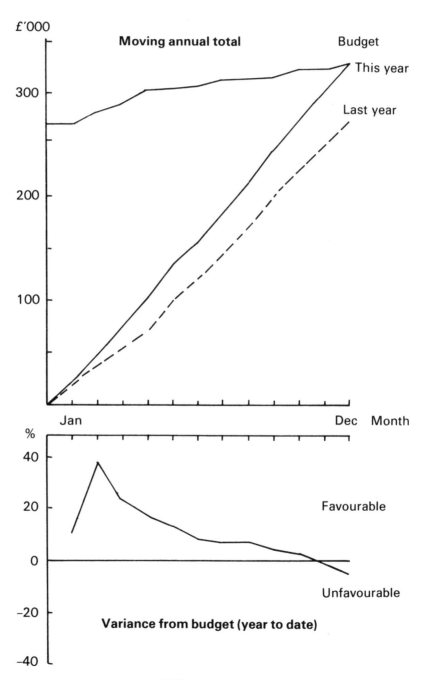

£'000

Moving annual total   Budget

This year

300

Last year

200

100

Jan   Dec   Month

%

40

20   Favourable

0

                                        Unfavourable

-20   **Variance from budget (year to date)**

-40

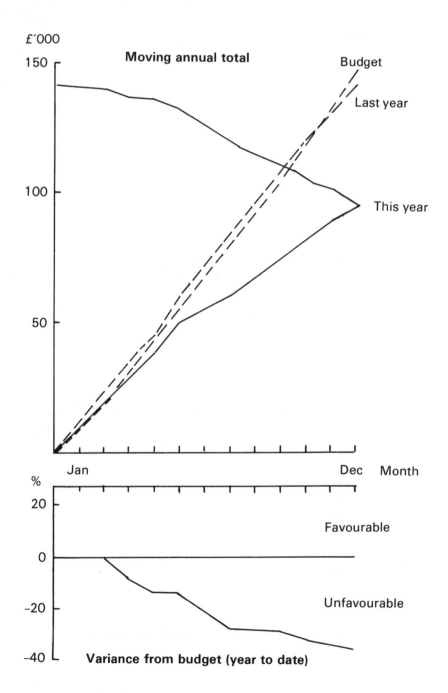

£'000

Moving annual total

Budget

Last year

This year

Jan   Dec   Month

%

Favourable

Unfavourable

Variance from budget (year to date)

**ACTUAL AND CUMULATIVE
SALES, AND MOVING ANNUAL
TOTAL: EXPORT MARKET**

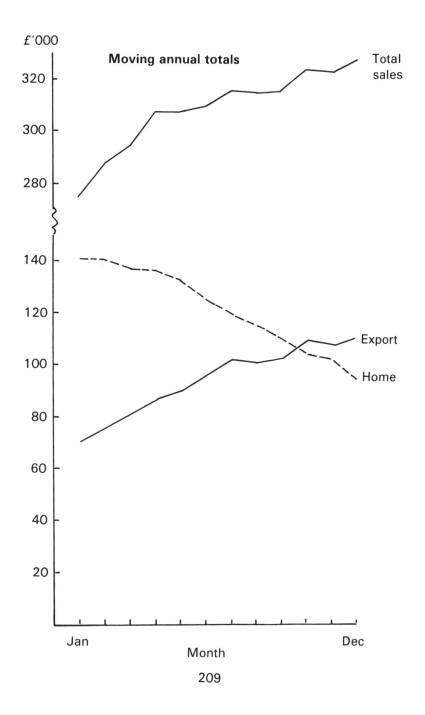

£'000

Moving annual totals

Total
sales

Export

Home

Jan   Dec

Month

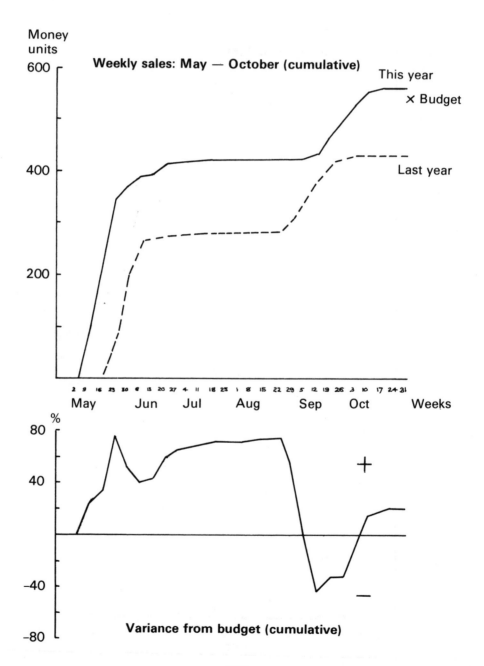

Money
units

Weekly sales: May — October (cumulative)

This year

× Budget

Last year

600

400

200

2 9 16 23 30 6 13 20 27 4 11 18 25 1 8 15 22 29 5 12 19 26 3 10 17 24 31

May   Jun   Jul   Aug   Sep   Oct   Weeks

%

80

40

+

−40

−

−80

Variance from budget (cumulative)

Data for graphical presentation on Data sheets 34, 35 and 36

	Data sheet 34		Data sheet 35				Data sheet 36			
	Company profit* (£'000), moving annual total		Profit margin† (actual as percentage of sales), moving annual average				Capital turnover (actual sales/capital), moving annual total, times			
	Actual	Budget	Com-pany	Div. A	Div. B	Div. C	Com-pany	Div. A	Div. B	Div. C
Jan	416	Detailed	13.6	18.3	10.4	13.1	0.99	1.19	0.74	2.19
Feb	418	in	13.5	17.9	10.5	13.3	0.99	1.22	0.73	2.18
Mar	420	accordance	13.4	17.1	10.5	13.7	1.00	1.23	0.73	2.14
Apr	426	with	13.2	16.5	10.3	13.9	1.02	1.30	0.72	2.22
May	431	agreed	13.3	16.7	10.2	14.4	1.01	1.24	0.71	2.22
Jun	438	budget	13.2	16.4	10.5	13.2	1.03	1.25	0.70	2.25
Jul	449		13.1	15.8	10.4	13.5	1.05	1.29	0.70	2.29
Aug	460		12.9	14.4	10.5	14.2	1.08	1.36	0.71	2.22
Sep	464		12.8	14.0	10.6	14.2	1.08	1.36	0.69	2.28
Oct	484		13.1	13.9	10.7	15.3	1.09	1.35	0.67	2.29
Nov										
Dec	520									

*Before taxation

†Before interest and taxation, shown as 'Combined Divisions' on data sheet

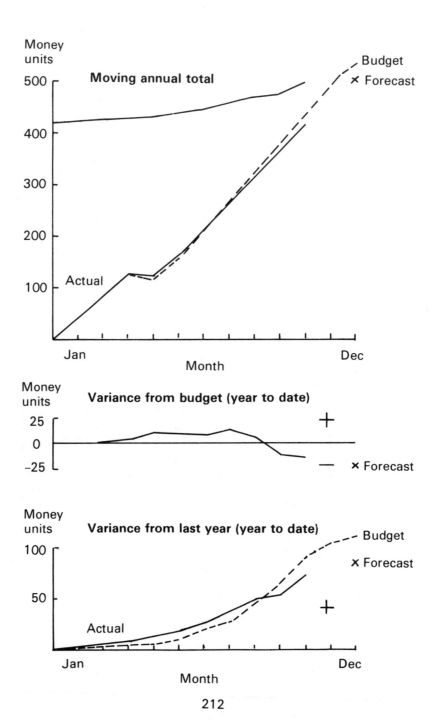

Money units

Moving annual total

Budget
✕ Forecast

500

400

300

200

100

Actual

Jan

Month

Dec

Money units

Variance from budget (year to date)

25

0

−25

+

──── ✕ Forecast

Money units

Variance from last year (year to date)

100

Budget

✕ Forecast

50

Actual

+

Jan

Month

Dec

212

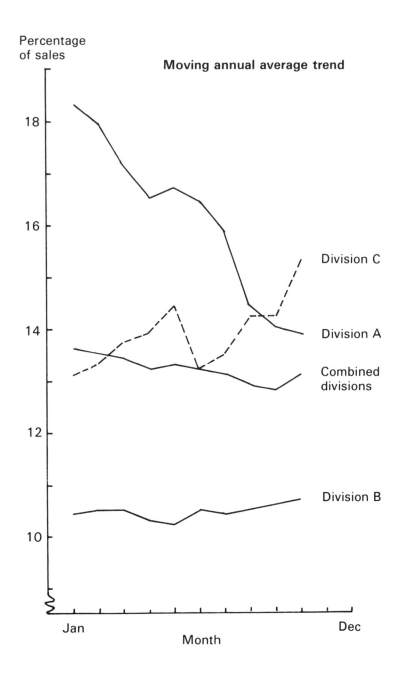

Percentage
of sales

Moving annual average trend

18

16

Division C

14

Division A

Combined
divisions

12

Division B

10

Jan   Dec

Month

213

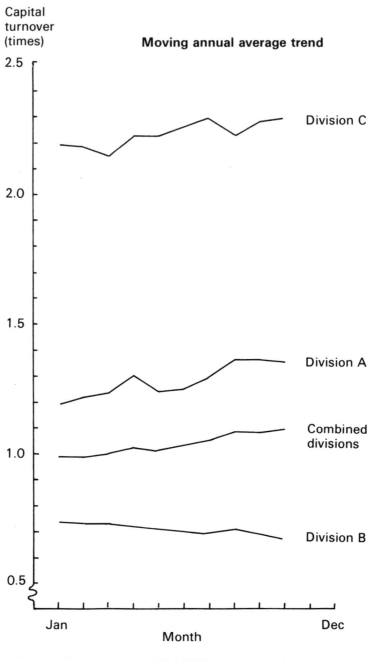

Capital
turnover
(times)

Moving annual average trend

2.5

Division C

2.0

1.5

Division A

Combined
divisions

1.0

Division B

0.5

Jan   Dec

Month

214

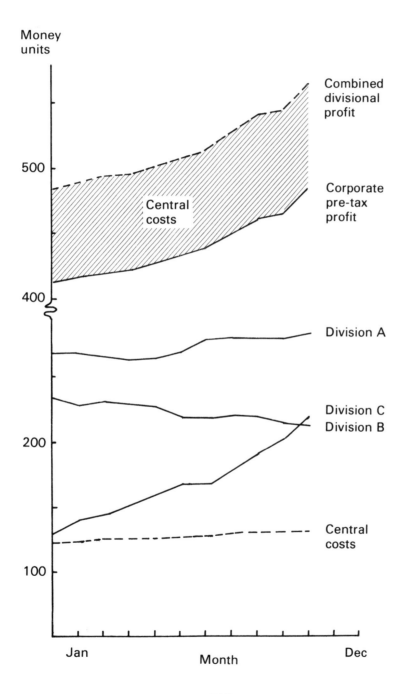

Data sheet 37
COMPANY AND DIVISIONAL
PROFIT TREND

Money
units

Combined
divisional
profit

500

Central
costs

Corporate
pre-tax
profit

400

Division A

Division C
Division B

200

Central
costs

100

Jan

Month

Dec

215

SUMMARY OF OPERATING STATEMENT	Company or business division:								

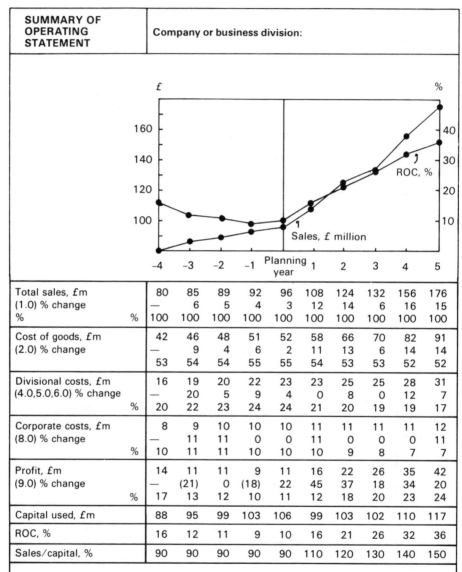

		-4	-3	-2	-1	Planning year	1	2	3	4	5
Total sales, £m		80	85	89	92	96	108	124	132	156	176
(1.0) % change		—	6	5	4	3	12	14	6	16	15
%	%	100	100	100	100	100	100	100	100	100	100
Cost of goods, £m		42	46	48	51	52	58	66	70	82	91
(2.0) % change		—	9	4	6	2	11	13	6	14	14
		53	54	54	55	55	54	53	53	52	52
Divisional costs, £m		16	19	20	22	23	23	25	25	28	31
(4.0,5.0,6.0) % change		—	20	5	9	4	0	8	0	12	7
	%	20	22	23	24	24	21	20	19	19	17
Corporate costs, £m		8	9	10	10	10	11	11	11	11	12
(8.0) % change		—	11	11	0	0	11	0	0	0	11
	%	10	11	11	10	10	10	9	8	7	7
Profit, £m		14	11	11	9	11	16	22	26	35	42
(9.0) % change		—	(21)	0	(18)	22	45	37	18	34	20
	%	17	13	12	10	11	12	18	20	23	24
Capital used, £m		88	95	99	103	106	99	103	102	110	117
ROC, %		16	12	11	9	10	16	21	26	32	36
Sales/capital, %		90	90	90	90	90	110	120	130	140	150

Notes:
1 ROC (return on capital) is before interest and tax.
2 Percentage change refers to previous year.
3 When used for a business division, omit corporate costs unless allocated.

216

Cross-index with
The Businessman's Complete Checklist

As well as being an index to this book, the following index gives cross-references with *The Businessman's Complete Checklist* (by W. C. Shaw and G. Day, published by Business Books) in which additional information can be obtained on the subjects indicated.

References to sections in *The Businessman's Complete Checklist* are given in square brackets, [], to Unit 1 of this book in plain numbers, to Unit 2 in parentheses, (), and for Unit 3 the numbers are preceded by DS (for 'Data sheet').